For Dale —

God bless!

THE WIT &
WISDOM OF
CAL THOMAS

PROMISE
PRESS

An Imprint of Barbour Publishing

Published by Promise Press, an imprint of Barbour Publishing, Inc., P.O. Box 719, Uhrichsville, Ohio 44683, www.promisepress.com

Member of the
Evangelical Christian
Publishers Association

Printed in the United States of America.

*Wit is folly unless a wise man
hath the keeping of it.*

—JOHN RAY (1627–1705),
English Proverb

. . .

If any of you lacks wisdom,
let him ask of God.
—James 1:5

CONTENTS

FOREWORD
by Dr. Laura Schlessinger

This book should be called *Essence of Cal*. Although it covers a lot of ground, it does so succinctly, with no loss of Cal's characteristic humor and ironic style. To wit: in speaking about the past he says, "Things were cheap then. Life was valuable. Now, life is cheap and things are valuable." See what I mean? "Bitter" sweet and to the point.

I must confess, right off the bat, that I am not objective when it comes to Cal Thomas. In the first place, we are friends. He even has some nice things to say about me in this book. In the second place, we share a conservative outlook on most things. (I cheered when I read in this book that "God is the author of marriage.") Perhaps, most importantly, we are unashamed of the fact that belief in G-d* and the practice of our different religions is what gives meaning and purpose to our lives. We also believe that the Ten Commandments are the foundation of the American Bill of Rights and Constitution, and deplore the rampant misrepresentation and misunderstanding of the concept of separation of Church and State in the 21st century.

Every important aspect of our culture and our society is noted in this book. Social trends and movements are linked to reveal the basic challenges to our national evolution. The disrespect for the value of life reflected by the rising number of abortions is taken to its logical conclusion with the growing advocacy movement for euthanasia. The indifference to

---

* *A note to those who are not Jewish. . . Orthodox Jews hold God's name in such high esteem that they do not fully spell it out, except when directly quoting someone else who is referring to God.*

family and the abdication of parental responsibility is revealed as the cause for wide-scale disrespect for authority.

Cal plays fair. Virtually every American institution is subjected to his X-ray vision, and most display signs of disease and decay, due in no small measure to the stranglehold that political correctness has on government, media, academe, and even our churches and synagogues. But he has the guts to place the blame where it belongs—right on your shoulders and mine. As I often say to my radio audience: "This is a country by the people, of the people, and for the people, and, baby, we BE the people!"

He exhorts those of us who value life, who believe in G-d, and who live by the Ten Commandments to accept responsibility for not only ourselves, but also our nation and our world. If we want to see a more godly country, more selfless politicians, more integrity, and more virtue in our society and its institutions, we must become lawyers, university administrators, moviemakers, etc. We must do the work and make the sacrifices to change society from within.

As Cal so eloquently says, "Changing a nation will take a change of heart and mind. . .no politician can legislate that."

Make no mistake. America is at war with its own principles, its own history, its own glorious goals. We must all enlist in this fight. Victor Frankel, another man I greatly respect, said, "Evil triumphs when good men do nothing."

This book is a clarion call to all of us who cherish traditional ideals and values. It exhorts us to stop complaining and stop expecting others to do the heavy lifting. There was a '60s slogan that said, "America, Love It or Leave It." Cal Thomas says, "America, Love It or Lose It."

ACKNOWLEDGMENTS

- I am delighted to welcome Wayne Stayskal, *The Tampa Tribune's* excellent political cartoonist, back for a second collaboration. Wayne and I teamed up in our 1985 book, *Liberals for Lunch.*

- Thanks to my cat, "Precious," also affectionately known as "The Wiener" for the sleek body she had when young (too much food and love have turned her into a full-figured feline) for posing with me on the cover. She is thinking of retaining an agent for future royalties and movie rights. Her role model is Morris the cat.

INTRODUCTION

Why a book called *Wit and Wisdom,* especially by me?

It's my way of getting back at all of those people who write in response to my syndicated column and call me a half-wit, dimwit, or nitwit.

In seventeen years of column-writing and many more years of appearing on television and radio and speaking in public, I have never thought of excerpting some of my thoughts for a book. But when Promise Press took to the concept that had been wandering around in the corridors of my brain, I pulled a collection of these thoughts out of the file and, with the able help of the writer Dan Pollock (who has served me well as an editor of these lines), have assembled something I hope will be of interest to many and of use to at least a few. Since "there is nothing new under the sun," as Solomon writes in Ecclesiastes (a humbling thought), no doubt someone has already "thunk" every thought contained herein. But perhaps I have managed to rephrase some of these ancient ideas for modern times in a way that might appear original. And there are, sprinkled throughout, the thoughts of far wiser and funnier men and women whose literary company I am flattered to keep.

Most conservatives are stereotyped as being humorless and full of everything but joy. That allegation is sometimes justified because we seem always to be against more things than we are for. I hope you'll find sufficient positive things and even some laughs in this book. These thoughts are intended not only for your own edification and enjoyment, but to be used in conversation, arguments, and correspondence to impress your friends as to how smart you are.

This stuff probably won't make its way into either Bartlett's *Familiar Quotations* or the *Oxford Book of Quotations*. If it did, I wouldn't need to put together this book. I hope you enjoy it. Drop me a note and tell me what you think, but if you think it pretentious or don't like it for other reasons, try to avoid the "nitwit" and "dimwit" stuff. It's already been done.

Cal Thomas

PART ONE

*The State of
the Nation
and the Soul*

CAUGHT IN THE CROSSFIRE:
LIBS VS. CONS

"Conservatives take account of the whole man,
while the liberals tend to look only
at the material side of man's nature."
—Barry Goldwater
(in *Conscience of a Conservative*)

Former talk show host Phil Donahue once said to me: "The problem with you conservatives is that you have simple answers to complex problems." I replied: "The problem with you liberals is that you've ignored the simple answers and that's why the problems have become complex."

For liberal Democrats,
it is always more blessed
to take and then deceive.

Senator Ted Kennedy has one major advantage over conservatives. The press never dubs him an "ideologue" or employs the modifiers "arch" or "ultra" as they do with conservatives who won't budge on their principles. Kennedy is portrayed as noble for not wavering. When they do the same, conservatives are called "rigid" and "uncompromising."

Conservatism has many obstacles to overcome, not the least of which is the stereotype of "mean-spiritedness" and "selfishness."

Some Republican governors are embracing "compassionate conservatism" with all the zeal of a New Age hugger. In fact, real conservatism is compassionate because it frees people from strangling government regulations, high taxes, and oppressive bureaucracy, allowing them to develop to their full potential.

REVERENCE FOR LIFE

ABORTION AND THE RIGHT TO LIFE

"Woe to those who call evil good and good evil."
—Isaiah 5:20

The *Chicago Tribune* reported on a conference of scientists meeting in Montreal in 1977 to study the latest research on DNA: "The overriding message of all this new research is that the life of a baby begins at conception."

Legal abortion was conceived in a lie. Norma McCorvey, "Jane Roe," claimed to have been raped. She later admitted lying in order to make her case more compelling to the Supreme Court.

The real extremists in this debate are those who have never met an abortion they would not prevent.

Women, who have for so long been lied to about so

many things, especially abortion, will be told by Democrats that only their party can best serve women's interests. Has it ever been in the best interest of women to kill their unborn children?

Justice Sandra Day O'Connor said the Nebraska law was unconstitutional because it failed to include a "health-of-the-mother" exception. That is a loophole large enough for any abortionist. Besides, how can a woman be a mother unless the child she has chosen to kill is a baby before it is born?

Pro-choicers prefer that abortions be shrouded in euphemisms and morally obtuse medical terminology and kept behind closed doors to spare the conscience and the soul.

*Loretta Young's car displayed
a bumper sticker that said,
"Your mama was pro-life, dawlin'."*

More than a century ago, the Supreme Court, which now denies protection to unborn life, denied protection to born life when the color of the human skin was darker than that of the majority. As with the unborn today, the Supreme Court then could not argue that the persons to whom they were denying rights looked human in every respect, so they had to claim African slaves were not "fully" human. With the unborn, the modern Court has said much the same, declaring developing humans not "persons." What's the moral, even legal difference? To reverse the former decision, a Civil War was fought. The outcome of our own struggle over life and death has yet to be determined.

In the '60s, I worked for NBC News in Washington. That network properly aired film of civil rights demonstrators who were sometimes beaten, shot with powerful water hoses and guns, cattle-prodded, and occasionally murdered. The power and reality of those pictures stunned the nation and changed hearts about the outrages perpetrated against black Americans. Now, when political people attempt to air commercials about another civil rights issue—the right of a nearly born baby to be allowed to complete the trip down the birth canal without being killed—they are told their language describing the procedure is "a little too graphic." Had network executives felt this way in the '60s, there would have been no civil rights legislation, or it would have been delayed, because the public would not have been fully informed about the nature and depth of discrimination and racial hatred.

The Freedom of Access to Clinic Entrances Act (FACE), passed in 1994 by a Democratic Congress and signed by a Democratic president, unfairly singles out a single issue—abortion—and makes certain forms of protest against it a federal crime. Yet no federal restrictions were placed on blocking the South African Embassy in Washington during anti-apartheid demonstrations. If such a law had been in place during the civil rights movement, owners of segregated lunch counters could have sued for damages to their businesses by black customers who were refused service and would not leave. Vietnam War protesters might have been fined for occupying government buildings or sitting in at Dow Chemical, a company that made napalm used in bombs that burned the skin off human beings, as certain abortion procedures burn the skin off unborn babies.

Killing a baby at an earlier stage does nothing to quell the moral argument, especially if the woman who uses the drug puts her own health in danger and if her mothering and nurturing instincts are further dulled by a "pill."

How can opponents of the death penalty who favor "choice" when it comes to abortion reconcile their conflicting positions?

Why be shocked when another young woman leaves her school prom to deliver a baby in the restroom, sees it drown in the toilet, and returns for the next dance as if emptying her womb and emptying her bladder are morally equivalent?

In 1977 the Reverend Jesse Jackson wrote an article for *National Right to Life News* that said: "It takes three to make a baby: a man, a woman, and the Holy Spirit. What happens to the mind of a person, and the moral fabric of a nation, that accepts the aborting of the life of a baby without a pang of conscience? What kind of a person and what kind of a society will we have twenty years hence if life can be taken so casually?" Those questions remain valid, though Jackson no longer asks them.

Thankfully, the woman Jackson impregnated was pro-life, at least regarding this child. Jackson, himself the product of an out-of-wedlock conception, is radically "pro-choice." He even opposes legislative attempts to restrain the procedure known as "partial-birth abortion," which sucks the brains out of a fully formed baby in the process of emerging from the birth canal. He says he loves the child he recently fathered, which makes one wonder if others might not come to love children conceived in difficult situations if those babies were allowed the privilege of their endowed right to life. None of us has control over the circumstances of our conception.

Today there is assistance—financial and emotional—for every woman with an unplanned pregnancy, so "freedom" is no longer the issue (if it ever was). The question is whether a pregnant woman will put her short-term self-interest on hold to take the long view and bless her child. A woman bestows no greater gift than life.

A national hotline, media campaigns giving new visibility to pregnancy-help centers, testimonials from women who have decided to deliver their babies in difficult circumstances and from those who had abortions and regret it—all these can focus the issue on women and their cares and concerns. If the abortion debate is to be turned around in favor of life, it will be with a positive, incremental approach aimed at helping women.

Help is available for women
with problem pregnancies.
Now all the women and babies need
is someone to speak for them.

It is not enough to support a constitutional amendment banning abortion. We must, in greater numbers, provide young women in trouble with a home and a sympathetic ear.

Some pro-life pregnancy centers are adopting a positive new strategy to save the lives of babies and the souls of women even in the midst of an abortion-minded culture. Many of these centers are being transformed into medical clinics where sonograms allow pregnant women to see inside their bodies and gaze at another body. (I have met women for whom this was the defining moment in their choice.) They also learn about other options, including adoption, and the many forms of emotional and material support available, which the "salespeople" at abortion clinics never reveal because it might hurt business.

For the first time I can remember, an entertainment program *(Touched by an Angel)* mentions PACE, which stands for Post Abortion Counseling and Education, a nonjudgmental program for women who have had abortions and need help dealing with the emotional and spiritual fallout they were told they wouldn't have by the people who sold them the procedure.

EUTHANASIA AND
THE CULTURE OF DEATH

Once it is established that some lives are less valuable and less meaningful than other lives (as happened in *Roe vs. Wade*), the rest is merely who's next and how quickly we can move forward with the disposal process.

The culture of death, having been successfully imposed on the innocent unborn, is now being slowly but steadily advanced against the sick and the aged.

Increasingly, the law is being whittled away so that the elderly and infirm have less protection than they once enjoyed. One court recently decided that the Constitution contains a "right to die."

Those who would further dehumanize us must wipe away every vestige of what it means to be unique among living things. They began with abortion.

They continue with infanticide (partial-birth abortion), and now they wish to complete their task with euthanasia.

One category of life cannot be declassified without endangering others. If the unborn can be aborted, individually or "selectively," then why not kill the newly born and the elderly if they become "inconvenient"? If there is no God to govern in the affairs of men, then why shouldn't government or medical ethicists or public opinion be our god?

Roe vs. Wade has spawned a disrespect for all life. Now Dr. Jack Kevorkian plies his grisly euthanasia trade because Michigan authorities are not able to stop him. And the pressure grows at the other end of life to lower the cost of medical care by euthanizing the elderly and infirm when they become too much of a "burden" on society.

Death itself is undignified.
But assisted suicide is demeaning to life.
It isn't death that needs assistance.
It's life.

We are truly frogs in a kettle. The heat is being turned up very slowly, and we don't realize that we are boiling to death. The language is being rewritten to lull us into complacency. The rush to kiss the death angel began with "living wills." When attempts were made to allow doctors to kill "terminal" patients, they failed because the public found that too repugnant. The approach was switched to "assisted suicide" because this strategy would focus attention on the suffering patient and make the doctor a compassionate dispenser of help and comfort.

Great horrors do not occur overnight, nor do they develop in a vacuum. They begin with small compromises, unnoticed by most people. They advance on a wave of apathy, subtle appeals to selfishness, and a loss of God-consciousness. When man places himself in the supreme position of deciding right from wrong, it is a very short step toward deciding such things for others and forcing even people who don't agree to subsidize these practices with their tax dollars.

CAPITAL PUNISHMENT: VALIDATING LIFE

From where and from whom does a murderer get his right to hold on to life? Why does a guilty murderer enjoy more protection under the law than an innocent unborn child?

The principal reason our nation needs to maintain and carry out capital punishment is that it is the only proper way we can place the highest possible value on innocent human life. A life sentence, even without the possibility of parole, is not a proper punishment for someone who sheds innocent blood. Depriving one of liberty who has deprived another person of life is a penalty that does not fit the crime.

Some strong advocates of the death penalty for first-degree murderers are having second thoughts in the case of a Texas woman convicted of the ax murders of two Houston people in 1983. Karla Faye Tucker, thirty-eight, is scheduled to die by lethal injection February 3 (1998). Religious broadcaster Pat Robertson is one of those who has come to Tucker's defense. Robertson believes that Texas officials should spare her life because she says she has been born again. Rev. John Boyles of El Paso agrees. Boyles thinks that attention should be focused on what Tucker has become, not what she did, and that who she is now, not who she was fifteen years ago, is reason enough to spare her. . . .

To allow people convicted of past acts to be absolved by future acts would ruin what is left of the criminal justice system. One of the ancillary benefits of having a death penalty is to force the guilty to confront their Maker in this life before they meet Him in the next and to make peace with God. . . .

If all you have to do [to get a reprieve from death row] is claim you have been born again, "revival" will surely break out in the prison system, and, instead of filing petitions with lawyers, inmates will start sending letters to religious broadcasters and pack the prison chapels. There will be no way to discern which inmates are telling the truth and which are running a scam.

If Tucker has truly been converted, she has already received the only pardon she will ever need. (January 13, 1998)

CIVIL RIGHTS AND WRONGS

"Believe in God,
follow God's principles for building
strong families and strong businesses,
and all the rest will come eventually."
—Booker T. Washington

How about a new generation of black leaders with a track record of really helping people, instead of the bunch we have had to contend with, which is mostly interested in helping themselves to the goodies at the political trough.

Republicans should take up the challenge Democrats used to hurl at them. Let's fix American cities before we start throwing money at Africa. Let Republicans write not only a new Contract with America but an Economic Emancipation Proclamation for Black America. It was a Republican president who freed the slaves. Let this Republican Congress free all poor people, black and white, from economic dependency on government programs and spark a financial recovery in our cities by giving tax breaks to those who will return to blighted neighborhoods and stay for at least a decade. Racism exists. But the best way to reduce its impact is not to pass more laws or fund more failed government programs. It is to help rebuild the black family and liberate blacks not only from poverty but also from the white paternalism that is little different from the plantation—when slave masters said that blacks couldn't make it on their own.

NAACP Chairman Julian Bond said the "main mission" of the NAACP is "fighting white supremacy to death." Not rebuilding the black family. Not restoring a value base in the black community. Not using the expanding black middle class as a role model. Not helping young black men who are disproportionately fathering children out of wedlock, or populating our prisons, or winding up dead in drug deals gone bad. Nor does the NAACP see as its main mission the economic resuscitation of poor blacks by their own efforts. It cares only about fighting "white supremacy."

Bush acknowledged that "the party of Lincoln has not always carried the mantle of Lincoln." Neither has the Democratic Party, most of whose leadership in the South opposed civil rights legislation and one of whose governors (now senator), Ernest Hollings of South Carolina, ran a Confederate flag up the statehouse flagpole in the early '60s. It was the sainted Bobby Kennedy who, while Attorney General, wiretapped Martin Luther King, Jr.

*Let's stop the songs about overcoming
and start overcoming.
When that happens,
real healing and real progress
will follow.*

Putting the black family back together ought to be of greater importance than taking down a Confederate flag. But actually doing something to help needy people would bring success, and success is the last thing demagogues want. It costs them votes, political power, and money.

The politics of race gets the Democrats votes but does little for the people who need to be told that their salvation does not lie on the road to Washington. Race politics doesn't communicate that the poor among them can make it just as their middle- and upper-class black brothers and sisters have done —through hard work, intact families, and never accepting defeat as the final answer.

THE WAR ON DRUGS:
FROM HEROIN TO RITALIN

"Drug use is wrong because it is immoral,
and it is immoral because it enslaves the mind
and destroys the soul."
—Sociologist James Q. Wilson

Do those wishing to do away with laws against drugs have any irreducible minimums, and on what are they based? Or is everything negotiable, including moral principles?

If society views the human body as merely a more complicated evolutionary product than a cabbage, then, by all means, let's dispense with antidrug laws and save money for those of us who are not addicted, who have no interest in drugs, and who would like to take nighttime walks through our cities. But if our bodies are "temples of God," and if laws are for the purpose of restricting behavior that damages the temples of those who are not constrained by a higher power, then antidrug laws have merit.

"A true war on drugs would begin with a greater parental presence in the home and a deeper parental commitment to children."
—Cal Thomas and Dr. Edward Dobson
in their book, *Blinded by Might*

An entire generation has come to believe that any kind of suffering is bad. We have become intolerant of any form of discomfort, including boredom. So, rather than do the heavy lifting that comes with personal responsibility, we take a pill, snort, or shoot up.

Press stories tell of a growing number of children who suffer from depression and how parents and the pharmaceutical industry prescribe drugs as the solution. If drugs are used to alter the mood of a child, what moral authority do adults have to persuade a teenager not to alter his or her mood with marijuana, heroin, or cocaine?

Behavior problems at day care or in school are dealt with by prescribing Ritalin. Childhood depression and misbehavior are increasingly treated with medication. Pressure increases on the Food and Drug Administration to approve drugs for children that are now reserved for adults. Why are we surprised when so many kids turn to illegal substances, considering they have been drugged since childhood?

EDUCATION:
HIGHER AND LOWER LEARNING

"If a nation expects to be both ignorant and free,
it expects what never was and never will be."
—Thomas Jefferson

Just as self-evident truth is no longer self-evident,
or even truth, the common core of knowledge once
taken for granted as an essential element in a well-
rounded education at an American university is no
longer common, nor can it be taken for granted.

In spite of longer school years, a doubling of teachers' salaries, and dramatic downsizing in classrooms, one-fourth of American children cannot, or can barely, understand written English.

Americans fall far short of the rest of the world in knowledge of geography. We not only don't know about events in the rest of the world, we don't know where the rest of the world is. In 1988, the National Geographic Society commissioned a survey of the geographic knowledge of citizens from many nations. The American team came in last.

There is a growing awareness among parents and students that in too many institutions of "higher learning," the learning is more about lower than higher things.

Who should be primarily responsible for child development, the state or the parents? And whose values should be endowed in our children, the state's or the parents'?

The schools have long been one large laboratory for teaching liberal views of sex, the environment, and

rewrites of American history in favor of multicul-
tural education. That's why American schoolchil-
dren know less and less about their own land and
why they increasingly see America as just one nation among equals, with little to recommend it over
others.

*Apparently the universities,
having refused to impose
a moral code on students,
are now refusing to impose
an intellectual one as well.*

Just who are the real extremists in America? The ones
who want to reestablish concepts such as right and
wrong in our schools, or those who kicked out the
Bible and put in the condoms and weapon detectors?

Most Americans say they believe in God, but government schools have been ordered to pretend He
doesn't exist or is irrelevant to learning.

Why is God the only idea banned from government schools, while the demons that produce the beliefs of a Harris, a Klebold, and a Becker are tolerated, protected, even promoted?

In one generation, we have passed from the free distribution of Gideon Bibles to the free distribution of condoms.

It's time to ask whether many of our universities (and public schools) are committing fraud by promising a real education and delivering something entirely different. They certainly are overpriced.

The National Education Association has succeeded in promoting its own narrow agenda while working against the interests of most children and their parents, who find themselves trapped in a system from which there is no escape unless they have the resources to provide private education (something the NEA takes a dim view of and seeks to subvert) or home school.

SCHOOL COMPETITION
AND HOME SCHOOLING

A huge political battle is just beginning over school choice. Most people think American public education was here at our nation's founding. In fact, the early American schools were mostly religious, private, controlled by parents, and in competition with each other. The objective was to educate students, not establish an education bureaucracy and careers for teachers. The public schools were started in order to mainstream immigrants, inculcate them with American values, and erase cultural diversity for the sake of a united nation.

Once during the Middle Ages, disgruntled students at the Sorbonne advanced to the lectern, stabbed their professor to death with their quill pens, and wrote out their grievances with his blood. Now that's real education reform!

Surveys show a growing number of public school teachers have so little faith in the very schools in which they teach that they are sending their own children to private, often parochial schools. What do they know that the elites don't want the rest of us to find out?

No matter how good a public schoolteacher, he or she will always be required to teach the state's values and the state's perspective on subjects from sex to history and biology.

Concerned parents are wasting their time trying to reform a corrupt system. Parents should reassert control over their children's lives by pulling them out of the government schools. They should see that their children are educated according to their values and beliefs, teaching them the truth about history and every other subject the schools once taught but have now mostly abandoned.

Virtually every other monopoly has been broken up in favor of competition except public education.

President Bill Clinton and Vice President Al Gore claim to support public education. But when confronted with a choice, they chose private schools for their children while continuing to deny an equal opportunity to parents of lesser means and influence.

It isn't the computer wiring of American classrooms that will give students the tools they need to learn. It is the freedom of parents to send their children to the schools that they, not government, choose.

K–12 education is a $400 billion "enterprise," twice the size of the telecommunications market. And it's a monopoly. Government has broken up smaller monopolies on the correct theory that monopolies produce a bad product at a high price.

Why is it that the National Education Association is pro-choice on abortion but anti-choice on where those children fortunate enough to have been born should go to school?

Those who are part of, or politically beholden to, the education establishment are worried about home schooling and how well children who participate do. President Clinton thinks home schoolers should be made to "prove they are learning on a regular basis" or be forced to go to government schools. This is surprising, given that home-schooled children consistently score higher on standardized tests than their government-schooled counterparts.

The education lobby and its political allies don't want to open themselves to competition because they would lose their political power, and they are willing to sacrifice even the future of children in order to maintain that power.

In business, people responsible for such low performance would be fired. In education, not only are they retained, but they ask for and receive more money, subsidizing incompetence and institutionalizing failure.

The National Education Association and its allies know that the issue isn't education, it's politics. The only way children can be forced to believe what modern educators want them to believe—about themselves, America, and the world—is to trap them in these failed institutions.

Polls have shown that the poor, more than any other group, want the freedom to choose their children's school. Why must they be doubly cursed, first with their own poverty, and second with a system that doesn't offer their children a chance to get a proper education, which is their best ticket to prosperity?

If a mutual fund were performing
as poorly as public schools,
a good financial advisor
would recommend the client sell
and find a better investment.

Any system that fails to produce results after all of the time and the billions of dollars that have been poured into it doesn't need renovation. It deserves to be completely replaced with curricula that serves children first and the political and personal interests of unions and politicians last.

Competition would weed out incompetent teachers and pressure all schools to improve performance or, like any business, they would be forced to shut down by schools that perform better.

An estimated thirty cents of every federal education dollar are lost in overhead and never reach the classroom (another reason why proposals to spend more money on education won't improve performance).

Contrast the pursuit of excellence and unique personal attention that are the norm among home schoolers with what occurs in government schools, where the curriculum is often dumbed-down and nonacademic subjects take time away from acquiring real knowledge and the endangered species known as wisdom.

Census data show public schools have become the second likeliest place in America for a violent crime to occur. The solution to the violence problem is not trigger locks, but unlocking the public-school door so kids and parents can escape if they choose.

PARENTING AND FAMILY VALUES

"Your success as a family,
our success as a nation,
depend not on what happens
in the White House,
but on what happens in your house."
—Barbara Bush (as First Lady)

When a man and a woman decide that their family comes first and order their lives in ways that prove their seriousness, society will prosper and politicians will have neither the authority, nor the need, to run our lives.

Did we really think that "no-fault" divorce would bring no consequences to kids who take their parents' rejection personally?

When people get married, they should decide on personal goals before career goals. If a job interferes with rearing children properly, it is better for the career to suffer than the kids. As for rules, why do so many parents stop setting them or relax them when children enter adolescence? That's when limits are most needed. At the end of the child-rearing process, which would you rather have: a young adult you can be proud of, or one that brings you grief as you contemplate what went wrong from your corner executive office?

You can't "microwave" a young life like the dinners that overworked parents cook for their overstressed children. Children, like the best prepared food, require time, attention, and heavy doses of love.

Parents have fooled themselves into believing that two careers are providing for a child's "needs," when a child's greatest need cannot be bought with money or material comfort.

Our most pressing problem
isn't the federal deficit,
but a deficit of time and attention
that parents give their children
and each other.

Even though the culture doesn't affirm good parenting, think of it this way. Which would you rather hear at your funeral—your boss extolling you for your dedication to the office or your child praising you for your dedication to his or her life?

Parents give and should receive the blessings that come from the company of innocence in an age when that precious state is increasingly short.

We don't need more federal money for day care, as President Clinton has proposed. States are flush with unspent Aid to Families with Dependent Children funds, should they choose to use them. We need a tax cut so women who want to stay home with their children have that choice.

After Paducah, Kentucky, after Jonesboro, Arkansas, after Springfield, Oregon, and Columbine High School in Littleton, Colorado, the pattern is familiar. With chips on their shoulders, grievances in their hearts, and weapons in their hands, students who should be planning for life instead plot death. We await the psychiatrists' explanation, but don't we secretly know what it is? When you mix the ingredients for a cake, you get a cake. When you mix the volatile ingredients of corrupted culture, vulgar entertainment, and broken, loveless families, you get child killers. Government officials are making predictable statements. Look for some to suggest adding more gun laws to the thousands already on the books that didn't stop these shootings. Politicians are powerless; parents are not. Parents have the best chance of curtailing violence in the heart before it reaches the head and the hands.

No one needs to wait for politicians to make our families better. Each of us has the power to do that ourselves. If we are estranged, we can at least attempt reconciliation. If we have been out of touch, new technology, old-fashioned letters, and the telephone can enable us to renew contact. If there are grudges, we have the power to forgive, especially if we are the wronged party.

Good moral health is the result of a balanced life modeled by parents who stay together, do not work to excess, and take the time to teach their children at home, in church, and in private schools where the truth can be conveyed away from the reach of the government's increasingly secular influence.

Quality time with children is quantity time.

Parents aren't powerless. They can control whether there is television in the house and what is watched. If they make it a priority, they can have one family meal a day together and converse without interruption. They can live as models to their children. They can ensure that the kids are educated in the truth and not propagandized by what interest groups think passes for instruction. It's more difficult now than when I was a teenager, but it isn't impossible to set kids on the right path. It just takes the right, sometimes difficult decisions.

President Clinton proposed the politician's solution (to the Littleton, Colorado, school shootings). He wants more money for emergency teams "to help communities respond when tragedy strikes." He has it backward. What is needed are emergency teams to prevent tragedy before it strikes. Those teams are already available, and the only cost associated with them is time. They are called parents.

ENVIRONMENTAL FUNDAMENTALISM

"We must make the rescue of
the environment the central
organizing principle for civilization."
—Albert Gore (in *Earth in the Balance*)

Gore suggests in his book that the environmental threat is greater than any enemy America has ever faced. That's not true. The threat is Gore's radical environmental policies if he ever gets the chance to implement them.

So many political and theological liberals need a cause to substitute for their moral obtuseness on such issues as abortion and homosexual behavior. They've found it in the worship of animals and plants.

If conservatives are to blame for Waco, Oklahoma City, and Ruby Ridge, who is responsible for producing Theodore Kaczynski, the Unabomber? Liberals. Kaczynski went to an Earth First! meeting at the University of Montana where a "hit list" of "enemies" of the environment was distributed.

Environmentalism is usually associated with people of liberal political persuasion. Two of the individuals on the Earth First! hit list were killed by bombs mailed by Kaczynski.

Liberals denounce "redneck" rhetoric when it comes from the mouths of Bible-thumping preachers. Then they engage in a kind of environmental fundamentalism on behalf of their god, the Earth.

Why hasn't Kaczynski been labeled a left-wing radical environmental extremist? It is because "left" is considered good and "right" is considered wrong by the political and media elites.

Does anyone doubt the president and his friends would have been heard from if, instead of mailing bombs to technocrats, Kaczynski had targeted abortion-clinic doctors?

If environmental wackoism is seen in religious terms, it is easier to reject as fanaticism. While no one is for dirty air and water, fewer people should favor an imposed theocracy based on a philosophy that the earth is holy and that the environmental "gods" must be appeased.

The Clinton administration, always seeking new ways to expand the power and reach of government, wants to use "global warming" as a scare tactic to acquire more power for government and, as a side "benefit," propel Gore, one of the most radical of the environmentalists, into the White House.

The broadcast networks cleverly refer to "scientists" in their reporting on global warming, without making a distinction between those who accept the theory as fact and the many who do not. Neither do they mention that many of those who believe the world is heating up to dangerous levels have little or no expertise in climatology or environmental science. It is comparable to receiving an opinion on your heart from an orthopedic surgeon instead of a cardiologist. Both are doctors, but only one is an authority on the heart.

Since the "cranberry scare" of 1959, through hyperbole about red dye No. 2, DDT, cyclamates, coffee, saccharin, electric blankets, video display terminals, benzine in Perrier water, amalgam dental fillings, cell phones "causing" brain cancer, and so much more, bogus science and government have teamed up to scare and intimidate people into believing the doctrine of a terminally ill planet absent the intervention of lawmakers and regulators.

GAY RIGHTS
AND THE HOMOSEXUAL AGENDA

"It is wrong to hate homosexuals;
and those who lift a violent hand against them
invite the wrath of God upon themselves.
Reciprocally, it is wrong for homosexuals
to hate Christians
or others who believe homosexuality to be a sin.
It is doubly shameful to aim
violent and destructive actions at these believers."
—The Reverend Jerry Falwell

If gay "marriage" becomes possible, then there is nothing stopping polygamists or anyone else seeking redress of unique grievances. Where will the line be drawn, who will draw it, and on what standard will it be based?

*God is the Author of marriage,
not a university sociologist
or think tank, and certainly
not the courts.*

Homosexuals get laws protecting not only their behavior, but they get to propagate their way of life as normal in public schools and in our culture. Meanwhile, the same courts deny those who disagree with them the right to pass laws that sustain a moral code in which they believe.

The Clinton administration has formally designated AIDS a threat to our national security. While the administration seeks to change behavior when it comes to teen smoking and putting trigger locks on guns, in the case of AIDS, it looks for ways to allow people to continue their behavior while avoiding its consequences, rather than suggesting they can change. Much of this has to do with the increasing influence of the gay rights lobby.

Gay rights activists refuse to debate a fundamental question: Can anyone change an attitude, a lifestyle, a form of behavior? Or are only homosexuals unique in that they have been programmed in a singular way?

To acknowledge that even one person can become celibate or convert from a homosexual pattern of behavior to a heterosexual one undermines the arguments gay rights activists have been making in favor of their "once gay, always gay" theory. Countering the conservative ads, gay rights groups are quoting people who claim they tried to change but relapsed. This is as persuasive as saying once a smoker, always a smoker. Why should homosexuality enjoy a category unique among behavioral patterns? The answer is politics and power.

It is true that some homosexuals revert to their former behavior patterns after testifying to being converted. But many have remained converted and feel liberated in their new, nonhomosexual lifestyles. Why don't we see more reports about the successes and not just the failures?

Rather than debate the issue on evidence, gay rights activists wear down a morally exhausted society that shrinks at the prospect of being thought uneducated, lacking in compassion, and judgmental.

Radio talk-show host Dr. Laura Schlessinger was on the fence about homosexuality until the gay rights movement pushed her into opposition when she failed to measure up to their lockstep requirement of unquestioning support for their beliefs, practices, and agenda. The slightest deviation can get you branded a bigot, mad, intolerant, nasty, and full of hate. She has been linked by activists to Hitler. Given her Jewish beliefs, that is a particularly outrageous insult that reflects more on the character of the insulters.

Dr. Laura may be a voice crying in the wilderness, but she's a loud voice and she isn't going to shut up. Attempts to silence her will have the opposite effect of making her even more popular. That's because she has something that is in short supply in the rest of the country, especially the increasingly gay-dominated media. She tells the truth and is courageous in telling it. We used to give awards and encouragement to such people. Now, as they are smeared as bigots, too many remain silent.

Homosexuals should not be censored, but neither should those who oppose their point of view. That's called free speech.

HISTORY: OUR ENDANGERED PAST

"By creating the impression that the new is
intrinsically superior to the old,
science and technology have effectively
dethroned tradition.
Simultaneously, they also elevated the stature of
the present and future in the human mind."
—Stephen Bertman
(in *Cultural Amnesia: America's Future
and the Crisis of Memory*)

*As we more and more find
the past a relic unworthy
of our attention,
our short-term memory grows shorter
and our ignorance grows larger.*

THE HOMELESS:
WHERE DID THEY GO UNDER CLINTON?

During the Reagan and Bush years, the press fixated on the homeless, strongly suggesting, and in some cases directly asserting, they were the fault and responsibility of Republicans and their "heartless" policies. The homeless disappeared as a group in the public mind about the time the Clinton administration took office in January 1993.

Mrs. Clinton said recently that the homeless who are mentally ill should be in institutions. Trouble is, some of Mrs. Clinton's ideological compatriots— civil liberties groups—two decades ago successfully sued and won the release of large numbers of mentally ill, drug- and alcohol-addicted people from the very institutions to which Mrs. Clinton wants them returned.

Seeking to exploit not only the homeless but the religiosity of the Christmas season, Mrs. Clinton has said that the baby Jesus was also homeless and that had He been born in New York City during the administration of Mayor Giuliani, He would have been mistreated. The record indicates that while

Jesus was born in a stable because "there was no room in the inn," Mary and Joseph had homes and presumably returned to them after fulfilling the purpose for their trip to Bethlehem—paying taxes, something that should please a liberal Democrat like Mrs. Clinton. It would appear that Mrs. Clinton's theology is as bad as her politics.

Liberal Democrats care about the homeless as much as Palestinian "leaders" care about refugees. In both cases, people are used as political tools to achieve the aspirations and enhance the power of their exploiters.

MARRIAGE, ADULTERY, AND DIVORCE

"There may be greater sins than adultery,
but not when it is happening in your family,
in your marriage, or in the marriage
of your parents."
—Psychiatrist Frank Pittman
(in the May/June 1998 issue of the
Family Therapy Networker)

The breaking of a business contract is more universally condemned than the violation of a marriage contract. Yet the consequences to a society which lowers its standards for such things are broken homes, broken children, and, ultimately, a broken society.

Elevating people with diminished personal character to leadership says that fidelity and infidelity are morally equivalent. That sends a message to the next generation that broken homes are no worse than intact ones, which social science and common sense tell us is not the case. While some think only about themselves, other lives are shattered and large numbers of children grow up without the unified family and role models they deserve.

Two of America's greatest problems—
divorce and illegitimacy—
cannot be solved by government,
only by individuals who
choose to live differently.

Which extreme should be held accountable for family breakup? Those who opposed "no-fault" divorce or those who supported it, along with prenuptial agreements and cohabitation?

THE SEXUAL REVOLUTION:
THE PARTY'S OVER

"For some on the extreme left,
unrestricted sex has become a sacrament."
—Gary Bauer

Now, four decades after the revolution began with Hugh Hefner's "Playboy Philosophy" (followed by *Cosmopolitan* magazine's Helen Gurley Brown's endorsement of sexual promiscuity for women), the casualties litter the battlefield. The "revolutionaries" probably won't accept responsibility for what they've wrought, and their contemporaries in the press are not about to hold them accountable.

Harmony and understanding, sympathy and trust abounding. It would be the Age of Aquarius. Because these people were more in touch with their inner selves, they would recreate the Garden of Eden where we all would live in perfect harmony with animals and plants. And they could engage in any sexual activity or living arrangement they liked without consequence. They thought abortion on demand was an answered prayer to their pagan hedonistic god. They forgot venereal disease, broken relationships, abandoned children (who as teen-agers commit suicide in record numbers), and a general decline in civility for which they are mostly responsible.

"The act of sex has complicated and profound repercussions. To deny this, to consider it to be something less special and powerful than it is, is a dodge and a lie.
Sexual indiscipline can be a threat to the stability of crucial human affairs.
That is one reason why we seek to put it under ritual and marriage vow."
—William Bennett
(in *The Death of Outrage*)

Many people seem to have forgotten about sin in an age where we are all supposed to be dysfunctional victims of someone else's wrongdoing.

We are so rapidly defining decency down that what used to embarrass us is now accepted and what once was "your ideal" is now embarrassing. Virginity and self-control are now mocked in an era when *Cosmopolitan* magazine encourages young women to have sex anywhere, any time, with anyone.

Worse than adulterous behavior is the growing acceptance of it by the public, if the polls are right. Women, especially, should realize that if they don't demand upright behavior in public men, they might soon be facing "downright" behavior in their own men.

God designed norms for behavior that are in our best interests. When we act outside those norms— such as for premarital sex, adultery, or homosexual sex—we cause physical, emotional, and spiritual damage to ourselves and to our wider culture. The unpleasant consequences of divorce and sexually transmitted diseases are not the result of intolerant bigots seeking to denigrate others. They are the result of violating God's standards, which were made for our benefit.

RADICAL FEMINISTS:
BEGUILED BY BILL

*Under Clinton, feminists have taken
the outrageous advice of some rapists.
They are relaxing
and apparently enjoying it.*

Immediately following Juanita Broaddrick's rape
charge against Bill Clinton, there was a deafening
silence from the National Organization for Women
crowd. Feminists have submitted to this president
and allowed him to abuse them for the cause of
abortion and gay rights. How anti-woman. How
pathetic.

Why should feminists ever be listened to again?
They have been accessories in Bill Clinton's raping
of America, its laws, and its virtue.

VALUES AND VIRTUES

"Purity of morals (is) the only sure
foundation of public happiness in any country."
—George Washington

A case could be made that our common values are
rapidly changing to the point where they are more
common than valued.

Cowardice has come at the point of attack against
foundational principles of right vs. wrong and
virtue vs. vice. Every victory by the forces aligned
against virtue has produced retreat and defeat by a
side that refuses to stand and fight.

When people spend more time trying to persuade
us they are honorable, rather than living honorably,
you can conclude their ethics are little more than
window dressing.

If a person has a private character problem, it will
eventually manifest itself in a public way.

*A person's character is produced
by his level of virtue,
and this is reflected in the ethics
by which he lives.*

If standards of measurement are tossed out, how do we know we are getting a true pound, quart, or yard of what we purchase? If moral standards are no more than what an individual or newspaper decides is moral at the moment, how do we know anything to be objectively true or untrue?

Why not validate everything? Think of how the crime rate would plummet if the illegal was made legal.

The worst thing in today's America is to say that one form of behavior or lifestyle is to be preferred over another. Test scores are being adjusted so that people can't fail. Some have suggested that no score should be kept in athletic contests so that participants would never feel the sting of losing. Some teams get awards just for showing up, thus diminishing the value of the hard work it takes to win.

The government and various activists believe we are all actual or potential victims of giant corporations that are so much more intelligent and sophisticated than we are that the Marlboro man or Joe Camel can persuade people who know better to suck the chemical equivalent of bus fumes into their lungs with no fear they will suffer harm. If the government had not been so insistent in tearing down the moral code that used to protect us in this country, perhaps more people might be able to judge right from wrong for themselves.

*The world may have changed
in fifty years,
but standards such as
integrity and virtue are timeless.*

For more than fifty years we have been subsidizing behaviors we once discouraged, such as sloth and indolence, irresponsibility, unaccountability, and sexual promiscuity. At the same time we've penalized things we once encouraged, such as marriages, hard work, entrepreneurial risk-taking, and innovation. We have done this not only in our social mores, but more conspicuously in our tax laws.

It can be dangerous to live in the past, but when something of value falls out of your vehicle, it is wise to stop, turn around, and pick it up before heading on. It is a metaphor for our hurry-up age that has lost something from our past but refuses to reverse direction and reclaim it.

Why did our parents'
generation fare better
with far fewer material things?
It was because their souls were
rich in the things money can't buy.

Then, a stained dress went to the cleaners. Now, it goes to the FBI crime lab.

Things were cheap then, but life was valuable. Now, life is cheap and things are valuable.

Thirty years of inattention to character, virtue, morality, and a definition of right and wrong have lead us to the present. A nation that has focused on physical fitness and changing the oil every three thousand miles in our increasingly expensive cars has ignored the societal "manual" that requires certain moral and spiritual "additives" if we are to enjoy an orderly society.

The boomers are, at last, growing up. And they are realizing there are certain truths about the human condition that cannot be ignored.

The focus groups are telling politicians that it's no longer the Age of Aquarius. It's the age of the serious. People are discovering that something is missing. The question is, are the politicians capable of giving the people what they need? Of course not.

CIVILIZATION AND CULTURE

"A culture maintains its identity by
passing on the sum of its values and experiences
from one generation to the next.
Its memory must be organic and transtemporal,
else the culture dies or survives
only as a hollow shell."
—Stephen Bertman (in *Cultural Amnesia:
America's Future and the Crisis of Memory*)

As a reading of history reveals, when a nation tolerates licentiousness, a culture quickly collapses.

The struggle to maintain what remains of the social fabric will ultimately determine whether we will continue to follow ancient Rome on the road to destruction or come to our senses, turn around, and reenter a harbor of safety ordained by God for our own protection.

Ten years ago I wrote a book called *The Death of Ethics in America*. If ethics died in 1988, what we are witnessing today is rigor mortis and the stench of decay.

Would they (the WWII generation) have fought so hard if they had known the traditional American culture would be shot down like so many planes by enemy fire?

Today's absurd rapidly becomes tomorrow's accepted, and those who once were revered by society for holding the line against advancing decay and decadence are now summarily dismissed as holdovers from a previous generation full of bigotry and discrimination.

"But neither the wisest constitution nor
the wisest laws will secure
the liberty and happiness
of a people whose manners
are universally corrupt."
　　　　　　　　　　　—Samuel Adams

When the sky turns dark during the day, it signals a coming storm. But what would be the signs of a deteriorating culture? Strangling inflation? An erosion of military power and influence? Corruption that is largely ignored? Rampant materialism springing from self-indulgence and an unwillingness to consider anyone or anything more important than one's own comfort and desires? How about children shooting each other in school? Would that get our attention?

*If there is disorder in the culture,
it merely reflects disorder in our souls.*

The old joke tells of the opinion pollster who asks a woman about ignorance and apathy. "I don't know and I don't care," she responds. That's us. But who cares?

"LAST SPRING YOU ROBBED ME AND GOT 3 YEARS. LAST MONTH YOU NAILED ME AGAIN AND GOT 5 TO 10... HAVEN'T YOU LEARNED YOUR LESSON YET?"

When people learn that life is cheap and thirty million (and counting) abortions prove it; when marriages split up at the first sign of difficulty; when violence oozes from every cultural pore; when younger and younger children regard sex the way another generation thought of recess; when violent video games graphically depict blood and guts; when evolution is taught as fact and humans see themselves as having no eternal significance or purpose; when any expression of public prayer or faith in God is treated the way cursing and contraband used to be, surely this explains why America has run amok.

Postmodern, aimless man says there is no evil because there is no God. If there is no God, we may do as we please. If what pleases some people hurts people we don't want hurt (with the exception of increasingly targeted Christians), then government steps in and fills the vacuum God has vacated. Is there a more plausible explanation?

The beast within us all must be bound by eternal moral laws, or it cannot be made to obey temporal, manmade laws. No law can be enforced, from speed limits to murder, unless substantial numbers of citizens are willing to obey.

MULTICULTURALISM:
"OUT OF ONE, MANY"

Instead of our national motto, "out of many, one," we are rapidly becoming "out of one, many." The strength of America is not in its diversity, as President Clinton and other multiculturalists regularly tell us. The strength of America is in its unity, its oneness. A rope is strongest when its many strands are tightly linked. A nation is strongest when those of many origins see themselves as Americans and not people of dual citizenship and dual loyalties.

The diversity proselytizers seek to divide, not unite. They're trying to create a "divided states of America," not strengthen these United States.

Taken to the extreme, America might come to resemble Bosnia, Northern Ireland, or the Middle East. Divided we fall.

POLITICAL CORRECTNESS:
INDOCTRINATION AND CENSORSHIP

"Bigotry," like "racism," is one of those bazooka words used by the protected classes to silence people who disagree with them. The prospect of being called a bigot simply because one has a different opinion intimidates television network executives, military commanders, politicians, and the medical profession, all of whom have tailored their beliefs and policies to avoid the brand of the scarlet or, in this case, the lavender B.

Then-Atlanta Braves pitcher John Rocker had used rough language to describe certain people who ride the New York subway trains and was disciplined with a fine and suspension by Major League Baseball. Perhaps Major League Baseball would do its players and fans a service by publishing a list of remarks it considers tolerable and which words will send the offending players to the sensitivity showers. For example, should a player blaspheme, will he be required to do penance to the offended religion? Players regularly question the visual acuity of umpires. If the blind are offended, would players be forced to walk around with blindfolds so they might be sensitized to how it feels to be visionless?

In Communist societies, when people say or write something that is regarded by the authorities as counterrevolutionary, they are sent to reeducation camp in order to get their minds straightened out. To facilitate the reeducation process, the reluctant camper is often subjected to physical and psychological torture. In America we have the same thing. We call it sensitivity training.

The Reverend Jesse Jackson was not pressured to take sensitivity training when he called New York City "Hymietown." When Nation of Islam leader Louis Farrakhan denounces Jews and whites, no one suggests he be sensitively trained. Were the Reverend Al Sharpton held to the same standard as John Rocker, he would be a permanent sensitivity-training camper.

At Vermont's Middlebury College, students, faculty, and administrators are debating whether to require the Middlebury Christian Fellowship to allow homosexuals to hold leadership posts. Would they dictate the doctrines of any other group? In other countries such forced indoctrination has been correctly labeled censorship and mind control.

THE THINGS THAT MATTER MOST

"How rich we are in things.
How poor we are in the things that matter most."
—Cal Thomas

In 1994 I published a book called *The Things That Matter Most*. I concluded the introduction: "What is required is for each of us to focus not so much on parties and platforms, and not on the agenda set by the cultural, media and academic elites, but on the things that matter most. In our hearts we all know what they are."

Following are some of my thoughts on these ultimate issues:

. . .

CHURCHES AND CHARITY

"Intoxicated with unbroken success,
we have become too self-sufficient to feel
the necessity of redeeming and preserving grace,
too proud to pray to the God that made us."
—Abraham Lincoln

Too many churches today appear more interested in preserving their programs and institutions than in taking on the role of servant, emulating the Leader they profess to know and follow.

A Roman official described the early Church to the emperor Hadrian: "They love one another; they never fail to help widows; they save orphans from those who would hurt them. If they have something, they give it freely to the man who has nothing. If they see a stranger, they take him home and are happy as though he were a real brother." There is power in that, real power. Why would anyone want to settle for less? The Church has the power to transform our nation into what most of us would like it to be.

The poverty industry has grown large and bureaucratic primarily because churches and their enormous membership have withdrawn from the privilege of serving God by redeeming the poor.

As the federal and state governments reduce their levels of welfare funding, churches, synagogues, mosques, and others like them must recall an earlier time when religious people were on the front lines in the war on poverty and the state was a last resort, not a first resource.

*If churches see the poor
as a burden and
the state as primarily
responsible for helping them,
they are rejecting one
of their fundamental
mandates and opportunities.*

One problem in fighting poverty is that people see the poor as a group and institutions as the solution. If the institution of government attempts to transfer responsibility for the poor to religious institutions, it will fail. The response to poverty must be personal, not institutional.

I confess to being double-minded when it comes to President Bush's plan to offer government funds to religious charities that provide social services. What concerns me is that religious organizations might be tempted, or forced, to dilute their life-transforming message in order to get government subsidies, thus negating the primary reason for their success. They also risk becoming an appendage of the party in power that financially smiles upon them.

There is a reason why it is more blessed to give than to receive. The receiver eventually spends his gift. For the giver, the dividends keep returning in the form of uncounted blessings. He also becomes an example for others to go and do likewise.

As we prepare to exit the twentieth century, we leave behind something precious from the nineteenth century—the few remaining societies and missions that once were the first line of defense against perpetual poverty. The reason is that they treated the poor and homeless not as incurable unfortunates but as redeemable humans.

For people who complain about
the cost and inefficiency
of big government,
volunteering even for one day
at a rescue mission provides
a blessing one cannot buy.

CHRIST AND CHRISTIANITY

"Preach the Gospel.
Use words if necessary."
—St. Francis of Assisi

Students are regularly discriminated against in government school when they are given assignments to write about their "favorite" or "most influential" person and they choose Jesus, only to be told He is the one person about whom they may not write.

As a pastor friend says,
we glory in the ritual
rather than in the Redeemer.
We cling to a shadow,
while rejecting the substance.

There are many Christians in other parts of the world who might gladly change places with American believers. In other nations they face torture, discrimination, and murder. Here, their "suffering" is limited to occasional slights from reporters and cartoonists.

Perhaps American Christians haven't been persecuted enough. They have had it too easy, grown soft and lazy. They relax in a subculture of their own making and are outraged when the world criticizes them. But they have refused to engage the world in sufficient numbers to make their influence felt in the very institutions they lambaste.

If Christians don't like being persecuted by intellectual snobs, let them enter law school, academia, the film industry, and journalism and change these and other fields from within. It's difficult, but not impossible.

For Americans, persecution occurs when the sermon runs past noon or a journalist calls Christians names. A Sudanese Christian might think Americans have it easy when their lashings come by way of the tongue, while his come from whip or gun.

Lighten up, Christians, and set about the business of doing the things that will bring real persecution. You're not being fed to the lions, but you are being fed a lot of baloney by some of your leaders who, frankly, don't know what they're talking about when it comes to real persecution.

America's most dangerous diseases have developed an immunity to politics. We suffer not from a failure of political organization or power, but a failure of love. In violent streets and broken homes, the cry of anguished souls is not for more laws, but for more conscience and character.

*No power on earth is greater than
a mind and soul reawakened.*

Every conversion is a miracle, whether the converted is a homeless person or a well-known figure like Jane Fonda.

*Nothing is more fulfilling than
witnessing a changed life,
unless it is watching
one's own life change
as a result of helping transform
the lives of others.*

CHRISTMAS AND EASTER

"It is good to be children sometimes,
and never better than at Christmas,
when its Mighty Founder was a child Himself."
—Charles Dickens

*Christmas and Jesus
have less and less to do
with each other
every passing year.*

Seeing how He has been eclipsed by a holiday that is pagan in origin and increasingly in practice, it may be time to separate Christ from Christmas altogether and for those who follow Him to take back what never belonged to the pagans in the first place.

Luke's Gospel records that the Wise Men brought expensive gifts to the baby. When He grew up, Jesus told us the only gift He really wanted was the gift of ourselves.

A Bloomingdale's newspaper ad features two gift certificates. One says, "Happy Chanukah," the other "Happy Holidays." What happened to Christmas? Was it thought some might be offended at the mention of His name even as part of a holiday, the true meaning of which has been lost in the shopping shuffle?

> *The hope of Easter is a rebuke*
> *to the faith of man in himself*
> *as well as to the idea*
> *of man's basic goodness.*
> *If man is basically good,*
> *Jesus died for nothing.*

Easter represents a seminal event in which there are only two choices. It is either the truth or it is a lie. There is no third choice on this one. If it is true, it changes everything, from the way we run our national life to the way we order our personal lives. If it is not true, nothing matters because, as the late Carl Sagan believed, we then cease to exist.

Former Watergate figure Charles Colson tells a story about why that scandal proves the Resurrection. He notes that it took only ten days after John Dean told Richard Nixon there was a "cancer growing on your presidency" before the first of the conspirators began copping pleas with the special prosecutor. Colson recalls that he and his colleagues were men of power who could order people around and get military planes to fly them anywhere. Yet, they could not hold a conspiracy together for more than a few days.

He then recalls Jesus' disciples. These were men with no power. They were attacked by religious and political leaders in an occupied land. They had no money or political influence. Yet every one of them went to his death, all but one a martyr's death, without recanting his testimony that Jesus was who He claimed to be. Human nature, says Colson, should have forced at least one to recant if he thought he was dying for a lie. Unless, of course, all of the events of those days were true.

According to the Princeton Religion Research Center's latest figures, about 170 million Americans now attend church on Easter. According to the Nielsen ratings, 128.9 million watched the last Super Bowl on the Fox network. If the real Easter story is true, then Easter is the real Super Sunday.

POLITICS AND RELIGION

"If you read history you will find that
the Christians who did the most
for the present world
were just those who thought most of the next."
—C. S. Lewis

Conservative evangelicals run the risk of depreciating their ultimate value, that of speaking for and building a kingdom "not of this world." There is precedent for what happens to the church's primary witness when it becomes overly entangled in the cares of this world. Look at the liberal churches, which long ago gave up preaching salvation (at least through Jesus Christ) and now mainly focus on political themes.

Conservative Christians ought to stop looking to the state for permission and validation and start looking to God for their commission and marching orders. If and when they do, they will find they are exerting real influence.

Conservatives are playing a dangerous game trying to fix "culture" from the top. They rightly criticize liberals for believing that government can cure virtually any societal ill. But are they any better when they attack the size and reach of big government only to call on government to reverse the immorality they see sweeping America? Government will reflect religious values when more individuals reflect religious values. But government can't make people reflect such values—it lacks the virtue.

"Religious conservatives,
no matter how well organized,
can't save America. Only God can.
But He will only consider doing it
if God's people
get out of the way and give Him room."
—Cal Thomas and Dr. Edward Dobson
(in *Blinded by Might*)

Suppose the Christian Coalition became known for transforming people's lives instead of trying to transform Congress, the White House, and the Supreme Court?

Abraham Lincoln may have had the best idea when he reportedly said that he wasn't so much concerned if God was on his side during the Civil War as he was concerned that he was on God's side.

A too-close association between religion and politics rarely causes damage to the state. The damage is caused to the church, because its primary message is obscured in the rush to crown a head of state instead of bowing before the King of Kings.

"It's easy to become enthralled with access to
places of supposed power.
In time, however, without even knowing it,
our well-intentioned attempts to
influence government can become so entangled
with a particular political agenda
that it becomes our focus;
our goal becomes maintaining our political access.
When that happens,
the gospel is held hostage to a political agenda—
and we become part of the very system
we were seeking to change."
—Charles Colson
(in *Who Speaks for God?*)

Conservative Christians aren't a threat to the state. They're a threat to themselves when they adopt the worldly tactics of those who appear to prefer political power to real power. One power changes occupants in Washington. The other changes hearts and lives.

*The church's existence
is not about building edifices,
political kingdoms,
or institutions,
but about building lives.*

There is a temptation some face today. Zealots wanted to overthrow Rome and take political power for themselves, using Jesus as their vehicle. Jesus says, "I am battling sin, not the Romans," something His contemporary followers might consider in their political alliances.

When a building's foundation is in disrepair, it must be replaced. Changing a nation will take a change of heart and mind that requires different behavior and better lifestyle choices. No politician can legislate that.

"If the Soviets could not kill the church,
what makes American
religious conservatives think
our government can restore it?"
—Cal Thomas and Dr. Edward Dobson
(in *Blinded by Might*)

PRAYER: PUBLIC AND PRIVATE

"I believe in the days before
theology the first prayer
offered by primitive man must
have been one of gratitude.
Like love and affection,
gratitude may mean nothing
to others unless it is expressed.
When it is expressed,
the effects can be miraculous."

—Steve Allen

Conservative Christians, especially, are fooling themselves when they think public prayers are a sign that all must be right with the world. Such prayers before football games do nothing for the quality of the game, and there is no evidence, nor could there be, of fewer injuries because God's name has been invoked over the loudspeaker. Furthermore, such prayers trivialize the act of prayer.

Public praying at football games is as incompatible as playing football inside a church building or piping an NFL playoff game into the sanctuary to persuade people to come to church on the Sunday of a big contest.

Some people think a lot of problems would be solved by hanging the Ten Commandments on classroom walls. Hiding them in our hearts might work better.

FREEDOM OF RELIGION

The purpose of the First Amendment, as originally understood, was that Congress would make no law establishing a national religion, so that everyone would have the widest latitude to freely exercise whatever faith they may or may not possess. But in modern times, the government has determined that the public square is to remain naked of religion.

When the Founders wrote the First Amendment, they largely sought to protect the church from government intrusion, not the reverse.

The study of theology is too much to expect in a nation that now regards what God says about anything as unconstitutional.

These days in America you are allowed to be "religious" so long as you do not take your faith too seriously. If there is a disconnect between personal faith and public policy, much of the public and all of the mostly pagan media will allow politicians to practice their "superstitions" in private. But if politicians seek to apply faith to public issues, they are labeled "religious fanatics" or, worse, "fundamentalists."

The left likes the policies of liberal leaders who invoke God but dislikes the policies of conservatives who operate in God's name. It isn't God they fear. It's the policies.

Some on the left would use religion to advance a social agenda underwritten by the taxes of all. They want its authority, but not its content. Some on the right use religion to advance a moral agenda through government edict, which they have decided is quicker (and more financially appealing and ego-fulfilling) than the selfless ways of the leader they claim to follow. To many of them, the way of the ballot box and the bank is to be preferred to the way of the Cross.

The acknowledgment by President Clinton's special counsel, Gregory Craig, that the president also has sinned is not news. Unfortunately, they don't have altar calls in the House of Representatives.

*When lawyers talk of sin
and preachers talk of politics,
surely the demons in hell rejoice.*

Race-baiting black preachers get a free pass from the media. So do liberal preachers who endorse their favorite candidates and criticize politicians from their pulpits—in violation of the left's sacred "church-state separation," to say nothing of the IRS Code.

SCIENCE AND RELIGION

God asks the ultimate question of Job that ought to be asked of evolutionary science: "Where were you when I laid the earth's foundation? Tell me, if you understand. Who marked off its dimensions? Surely you know! Who stretched out a measuring line across it? On what were its footings set, or who laid its cornerstone—while the morning stars sang together and all the angels shouted for joy?"

In our time, who in political and scientific circles is going to sound the warning that we should know the rules of the road and our destination before putting our trust in the human genome map, the scientists who can read it, and the politicians who seek to manipulate it for their own purposes?

Science can debase human creatures
when it treats us
as evolutionary accidents
with no intrinsic moral significance
and the state assigns itself
the role of God.

If God is impersonal, or does not exist, and if man is not made in His image, on what basis do we appeal to a racist who wants to deny blacks equal opportunity?

How quickly we have moved from a view of man as "an earthly animal, but worthy of heaven," as St. Augustine called our race, and a little lower than the angels, "but crowned with glory and honor," in the psalmist's words, to our present moment when scientists manipulate, extinguish, or preserve human life at any stage based only on their own personal goals and objectives.

As moral beings, we make choices and are responsible (to God and to others) for those choices. To say that our genes make us do this is a more sophisticated, but just as wrong, explanation for human behavior as the late comedian Flip Wilson's character Geraldine's: "The devil made me do it."

If genes explain some bad behavior, why not all bad behavior? Why stop with adultery? Let's ditch the Ten Commandments on grounds that God doesn't understand evolutionary psychology.

SECULARISM AND RELATIVISM

One of the dangers of secularism is that it does not give a person sufficient insight to explain what to a secularist seems unexplainable. Secularists have believed in the basic goodness of man. Secularists have falsely believed that if they do something nice for evil people, then evil people will reciprocate and either stop being evil or stop doing evil things. This is the ultimate in wishful thinking and denial. And it plays into the hands of evil.

"THEN, DEPENDING ON IF THE ACLU SUES US OR NOT, THE ANGELS WILL BOW AND SING 'SILENT NIGHT' OR 'RUDOLPH, THE RED-NOSED REINDEER'!"

"We're redefining in practical terms
the immutable ideas that have guided us."
—Bill Clinton

God does have a position on crime. He's against
murder and stealing, among other things. His position on crime is in the Ten Commandments, which
the not-so-Supreme Court (they haven't met the
ultimate judge yet) says cannot be displayed in government schools.

TELEVANGELISTS:
SEEKING GRACE OR GRACELAND?

Which is the more offensive image: Pat Boone in a modified heavy metal outfit or some overweight religious TV hosts who sit on overstuffed couches with makeup so thick it resembles a death mask and tacky sets that mimic the interior of Graceland?

*"Man looks at
the outward appearance,
but the Lord looks at the heart,"
says 1 Samuel 16:7.
Unless, of course,
you're a TV evangelist
who focuses mainly
on the bottom line.*

PART TWO

Washington and the World

THE PRESIDENCY:
LEADERSHIP REFLECTS FOLLOWERSHIP

Behold, my son,
with how little wisdom the world is governed.
—Axel Oxenstiern (1583–1654)

People ask me what they should read in order to keep up with everything going on in Washington. I tell them I read the *New York Times* and my Bible every day so that I know what each side is doing.

"It is a great advantage to a president,
and a major source of safety to the country,
for him to know that he is not a great man.
When a man begins to feel that he is
the only one who can lead in this republic,
he is guilty of treason to the spirit
of our institutions."
—Calvin Coolidge

Each presidential election cycle allows us to hold up a mirror to ourselves. The image we see is not the leader's face but our own.

Leadership reflects followership, and in what's left of our constitutional republic, the fault, to paraphrase Antony's oration in Shakespeare's *Julius Caesar,* does not lie in our leaders, but in ourselves.

A president's job is to call citizens to something higher and better than themselves. He can start with the Baby Boomers.

America was founded on optimism.
It flounders in pessimism.
Voters respond to a positive outlook
in which the one who would
be their leader
taps into the best in them,
not the worst in others.

All presidents, regardless of party, love to wrap themselves in men (and women) of the cloth, especially when their presidencies are unraveling.

PAST PRESIDENTS:

CALVIN COOLIDGE

"Mr. Coolidge had such a shield
in his demonstrated character that
political arrows fell from it blunted and broken."
—*New York Times* Editorial
(March 1, 1929)

Not only does the thirtieth president have much to teach modern politicians and citizens about the role and cost of government (he cut taxes four times and reduced the national debt by one-third while maintaining a surplus every year in office); we might consider the unity of his public and private character, which led to an administration and life unstained by scandal.

RICHARD NIXON

In spite of Richard Nixon's White House church services, the tape recordings of Oval Office conversations revealed him to be more gifted in the language of the devil than he was at utterances pleasing to the Lord.

RONALD REAGAN

"I'm not going to Washington to
make friends with the alligators.
I'm going to drain the swamp."

—Ronald Reagan

Reagan's strength was that he loved people, even his opponents. He kept his focus on the real enemy: wrong ideas.

Reagan wanted to rid the world of communism because he saw it as the ultimate impediment to the freedom we enjoy. He succeeded with the Soviet Union, and millions of souls breathe free today because of him. He wanted to reduce the size and cost of oppressive government at home, and he unleashed the greatest economic boom in history.

Reagan's greatest skill was transcending the media. His constant reminder was that real power does not lie in government but within each American.

Ronald Reagan's secret,
which nearly everyone misses,
was not only his ideas.
He restored the people's
faith in themselves.

The *New York Times* questions whether Reagan's 1981 "evil empire" speech, in which he declared economic war on the Soviet Union, "was the act of a simpleton or a visionary strategist." It was far more visionary than the *Times* editorial page, which regularly denounced Reagan for refusing to buy the liberal dogma of a nuclear freeze, unilateral disarmament, and accommodation with the Soviets.

"Reagan is probably the most underestimated politician of the post–World War II era."
—Lyn Nofziger

BILL CLINTON

> "For God's sake,
> figure out what kind of person
> we have here in the White House."
> —House Impeachment Manager
> Rep. Lindsey Graham (R-SC)

If many of us saw ourselves, or at least saw how we would like to be, in Ronald Reagan, Bill Clinton reflects who we really are. To indict him is to indict ourselves. His is a mirror that reflects our darkened souls.

An ideological kleptomaniac and a candidate of many colors, Clinton has no ideas of his own. For him, winning, not leading, was everything, and he did what it took to win.

President Clinton has prospered politically because he is like a parent who allows a child to eat his dessert instead of his vegetables to keep the child happy. Seeking such short-term approval leads to nutritional deficiency. Clinton's pandering to voters' feelings instead of tending to society's ultimate needs garners high polling numbers. And for him, that's enough.

It was said of Ronald Reagan that he had so much respect for the presidency he never removed his suit coat while in the Oval Office. Clinton respects it so little he has trouble keeping his pants on there.

Having shred his personal dignity, he also shred the dignity of the White House. He took the office nobly filled by Washington, Jefferson, and Lincoln, and turned it into a room at the Playboy mansion.

If the charges don't stick,
let the Senate acquit.
But if the charges are true,
censure won't do.

Although he personally approved a strategy to target donors who had given between $50,000 and $100,000 to the Democratic National Committee, the president told those assembled at his news conference that "there was no specific price tag to the coffees," and that he was "stunned" when he learned of the source of some of the checks. It's like having the piano player in a brothel tell the vice squad that he's shocked to learn what goes on upstairs.

Harry Houdini billed himself as the greatest escape artist in history. He never met Bill Clinton.

All of the blame can't be placed on Clinton. A con artist must have a willing dupe to be successful. He must have people willing, even wanting, to be told what they wish the truth to be.

When President Clinton starts talking about what is moral, as he did when recommending a national law banning human cloning, it's time for us to lock up our daughters.

As the most pro-abortion president in history, Clinton has no moral standing to speak against cloning. It would be like Pamela Lee, the *Baywatch* star who reveals her assets even while pregnant, coming out in favor of modest dress.

Since 1992, Clinton defenders have said that character doesn't count and that a president can separate what he does in private from what he does in public. But you can't subdivide character. The same moral (or immoral) compass that guides in public matters must also guide in private ones, unless scientists can clone an alternate conscience.

Former Democratic Senator Gary Hart of Colorado suggests that if we make marital fidelity a standard for leadership, we will have mediocre leaders. We've heard this curious claim before. It implies a correlation between promiscuity and leadership skills and mental acuity. If this is so, Bill Clinton probably scores as the greatest president in history.

The president is alleged to have told Lewinsky that oral sex is not prohibited in the Bible and therefore is not adultery. It's an interesting pickup line. But I wonder how the president might interpret this Bible verse: "Be sure your sins will find you out."

When King David of Israel committed adultery with the beautiful Bathsheba and sent her husband off to the front lines to be killed in battle, the prophet Nathan confronted the king and exposed his immoral behavior. This led David to confess his sins and repent. Today, David would have hired a good criminal defense attorney and used his palace staff to spin for him and smear the prophet.

Billy Graham said Clinton would make a good preacher. Like Jimmy Swaggart?

Had President Clinton not chosen politics as a career, he could just as easily have become a television evangelist. In his State of the Union address, the President was in the role of Jimmy Swaggart, preaching virtue while practicing deceit.

President Clinton says that if Republicans get their way on tax cuts, women will suffer more than men. He knows about suffering women. He's been responsible for inflicting pain on legions of them.

Bill Clinton has been a "good" father and husband, according to Mrs. Clinton, leaving us to wonder what would constitute a bad husband and father and how a man who has not had an affair would rate with her. Maybe she grades on the curve.

A truth-teller doesn't need a Hollywood producer to help him with body language and acting skills or to scorch the earth with the bodies of those who tell the truth about him.

The Clintons could expect media cover for some of their lies. But we have progressed to the "damn lies" stage, and the press has been forced to pay attention.

"If we tell the truth,
we only have to tell the truth once.
If you lie, you have to keep lying forever."
—Rabbi Wayne Dosick

Clinton doesn't split hairs. He splits rhetorical atoms. Reading through the transcripts of Clinton's testimony before a grand jury (or watching the tape) is an exhausting experience. He takes us on a semantical forced march at the end of which we don't know where we've come from or where we are. All we know is that we can't take much more, and we want to escape while we still have our senses.

*Once we realize someone
is a chronic liar,
we check our watches when
he tells us what time it is.*

Those who still defend this man for political reasons now call on the public to forgive him, though he has not made the request himself. But forgiveness without repentance is cheap grace. It says that what he did to himself, his family, and the nation is as acceptable as the behavior of those who remain faithful to their spouses and a good example to their children.

The credibility of repentance diminishes the closer one gets to being found out. In President Clinton's case, his came on the day the Starr referral arrived on Capitol Hill.

Clinton feels about religion the way he feels about sex. He likes the kind that makes him feel good but requires nothing of him.

The president is employing a trinity of "personal spiritual advisors" he says he'll meet and pray with weekly. He's also bringing in a new team of legal and political advisors. While one team thinks it can save the president's soul, the other team will try to save his behind. Church and State never looked worse together.

Our politics and our nation need a bath after Bill Clinton. Or perhaps an exterminator. Or, best of all, an exorcist, because the demons in him have invaded too many of us and are now an uncountable legion.

It's mourning time in America.

His behavior alone has brought forth on this continent a slimed nation along with the calamitous idea that all men are created lechers and that they have evolved with certain unprincipled rights. These include a right to abuse high office, lie to the public and their duly authorized elected and judicial representatives, and a general obtuseness to high and holy things in favor of low and debauched things.

President Clinton is guilty not only of contempt of court. He is guilty of contempt of country.

If the man didn't have bad character, he would have no character at all.

Clinton said he has promoted peace around the world and specifically mentioned the Middle East, the Balkans, and Northern Ireland, not one of which is seeing lights at the end of the tunnel. He took credit for more adoptions, while supporting abortion policies that will limit the number of babies available to be adopted. But as Professor Hill said, "I can deal with the trouble here with a wave of my hand, this very hand." And wave his hands Bill Clinton did.

What about Clinton's enablers, apologists, and defenders? What did they get for mortgaging their own integrity on Bill Clinton's altar of fertility? They got stained, as have all who came to his aid over the years.

Clinton still faces the judgment of history, but he has always lived in the present, even while singing "don't stop thinking about tomorrow," or reflecting his real philosophy of life, which is summed up in another song: "Let the devil take tomorrow, help me make it through the night."

GEORGE W. BUSH

George W. Bush is being coy.
Fame, not to mention the presidency,
may be about to start flirting with him.

(July 6, 1998)

Bush-Cheney may not be exciting, but after what this administration has put the country through for eight years, we could all use a little rest and some serious men with integrity in the White House.

SOME ALMOST-WERES
AND WANNABES:

BARRY GOLDWATER

"Mr. Conservative" was the
ideological godfather to Ronald Reagan
and the entire modern conservative movement.

NEWT GINGRICH

Gingrich's big mistake was to let the understandable euphoria Republicans felt in 1994, after winning a House majority for the first time in four decades, turn into triumphalism. A little humility goes a long way.

If Gingrich burns out, if the press and his opponents scorch him beyond recognition, so be it. Others will rise up to take his place. Besides, isn't a comet a dying star? (April 22, 1996)

The powerlessness of politics to reach into the heart was trumpeted by news that former House Speaker Newt Gingrich is divorcing his second wife. Reports say he has been having an affair with a congressional aide young enough to be his daughter. Gingrich and several other members of Congress won a Republican majority in 1994 by touting "family values." How can people who want credit for honoring the Contract with America be taken seriously when they violate a contract with their wives? If they won't impose "family values" on themselves, why should the rest of the nation accept them trickling down from Washington?

ALBERT GORE

"You have a vice president who
can't even recognize monks when
they're wearing saffron robes."
                    —Newt Gingrich

Under Gore, we'd trade in our SUVs for the transportation equivalent of Yugos. Unemployed people could be absorbed into environment-related positions that would promote the secular dirt gods with the zeal of Buddhist temple fund-raisers.

Displaying his theological ignorance (matched only by his environmental ignorance), the vice president said that Mary and Joseph were homeless. In fact, they had left home to pay taxes in another town.

To a liberal like Gore, all big things—from oil companies to SUVs—are evil, except big government.

The gap in one of Richard Nixon's surreptitiously recorded conversations with his staff was a mere 18 ½ minutes. The gap in Al Gore's e-mails is one year.

In his book, *Earth in the Balance,* Vice President Al Gore positions himself as something of a scientific expert. But on last Sunday's *Meet the Press,* Gore showed that he has an enormous hole in his moral ozone layer.

Gore says he's learned from his mistake and now knows how badly we need campaign finance reform. With that logic, Watergate might have been a learning experience for Richard Nixon.

If Al Gore winds up losing this election, I understand Tony Robbins is going to hire him as a motivational speaker. His topic: "How to almost win."

HILLARY CLINTON

"The pattern is clear:
rule-making for others,
rule-breaking for herself."
—Michael Barone
(*U.S. News and World Report,*
July 12, 1999)

Mrs. Clinton is an unredeemed '60s leftist. Her resume and writings reveal a philosophy rooted in big government and an antipathy to individual freedom, personal responsibility, and accountability. She wants to make government our keeper as well as our savior, and she will tax anything (literally and figuratively) to impose her utopian vision.

"Peter betrayed (Jesus) three times," says Mrs. Clinton, "and Jesus knew it but loved him anyway." Bill Clinton is no Peter, and she is certainly no Jesus. But the analogy is revealing. From the beginning, these two have seen themselves as the saviors of the world and those who oppose their agenda as children of Beelzebub. This is why they have been able to get away with so much. To oppose saints is to oppose God Himself.

We have moved to another level. The Clintons are beyond all accountability because, like the Blues Brothers, they are on a "mission from God."

THE MILITARY:
UNDER ATTACK

America's military power has always been sustained by our moral power. The world knows that we stand for certain principles, and, while we might sometimes make short-term compromises, with the exception of Vietnam, we rarely lose sight of our ultimate objectives.

Are we willing to pay the price
of a weakened military
so that politicians
and the gender feminists
can have their way in the
emasculation of our armed services?

The families of those in the military ought to be grateful we have leaders who anguish over the morality of war and the responsibility they have for the lives of others.

More attention has been paid to sensitivity training and diversity in the armed forces during the Clinton-Gore years than on the ability to fight and win wars.

The feminization of the military apparently means that fainting couches will need to be supplied along with more traditional gear. The military might eventually be forced to do away with weapons because someone will assert that "war is icky."

FOREIGN POLICY:
DATELINES AND DEADLINES

CHINA:
WAITING FOR THE DAY OF LIBERATION

"If China remains aggressive
and the United States naive,
the looming conflict between the two countries
could even lead to military hostilities."
—Richard Bernstein,
former *N.Y. Times*
Beijing bureau chief,
and Ross Munro,
former *Time Magazine*
Hong Kong bureau chief
(in *The Coming Conflict with China*)

The Chinese Communist government will be a growing problem for the United States in the new century. The Clinton administration's legacy may be that it restarted the Cold War just to perpetuate itself in office. The Chinese now have everything they need to make the world an unsafer place.

The president thinks he can fool China the same way he fools a majority of Americans. But the Chinese are tough cookies who have correctly read Bill Clinton's fortune.

*In considering China,
the left exhibits the same foolishness
it did with the Soviet Union:
a belief in "moral equivalency."*

The Clinton administration has even allowed Gen. Xu Huizi, the man who ordered the crackdown against pro-democracy students in Tiananmen Square in 1989, to visit the Pentagon's war room. Do we care so little about those who died and their cause—which used to be ours—freedom?

At some point the United States must stop behaving like a paper tiger and begin backing up its threats with action, or China will think it can get away with murder (which it did at Tiananmen Square).

When the Tiananmen Square massacre cost China nothing, when it saw our timid reaction to its intimidation of Taiwan during the island's recent presidential election, when China hears threats and sees no follow-up, why should it take America or this administration seriously?

Yes, China has one-fourth of the world's population; but does that mean America stands for human rights only in countries it can overwhelmingly intimidate?

On Friday (October 1, 1999), the People's Republic of China will "celebrate" the fiftieth anniversary of the Communist state. According to "The Black Book of Communism: Crimes, Terror, Repression" (Stephane Courtois, Editor, Harvard University Press), sixty-five million Chinese have died under the Chinese regime, as have six million Tibetans. The dead include those unarmed citizens massacred ten years ago in Tiananmen Square, the site where the military will parade.

Adding to this human tragedy and its affront to the supposed ideals of all free people will be the presence of many Fortune 500 CEOs. The color of money apparently is sufficient atonement for the color of blood spilled by the Beijing butchers. Whatever Friday's parade is, it ought not to be thought of as a celebration. Let's save the celebrating for the day of China's ultimate liberation, perhaps by the children of the bloody generation.

Communism can never be "gotten right" because its founding principle that the state is god is wrong. It survives only because aging dictators don't mind killing a lot of people to stay in power.

The reason communism will be defeated in China, as it was in Russia, is that communism has always ignored the depth of the human spirit, which yearns to breathe free and will not be stifled for long.

HONG KONG:
MRS. THATCHER'S PROPHECY

Former British Prime Minister Margaret Thatcher busily told all who would listen of her optimism that Hong Kong has less to fear from China than China has to fear from Hong Kong.

IRELAND:
THE COLOR OF MONEY

A tiny minority of lovers of violence and haters of people has held Northern Ireland hostage. It doesn't take that many if they've been carefully taught to hate.

Economic expansion may overwhelm this ancient religious-political conflict. There is a building boom throughout Ireland. New homes and roads are under construction and jobs are being created. Signs of budding affluence are everywhere, including in stubborn pockets of poverty in the south. For the first time in many decades, Ireland is seeing its native sons and daughters returning from other lands.

"Prosperity is a new visitor to Ireland," says the taxi driver. "She's not been here before." The Irish economy is booming, thanks mainly to the "supply-side economics" derided by big government devotees in America and by editorial writers for influential publications such as *The Economist* and *Financial Times.*

For those too young to recall the Reagan boom, or who have forgotten, or who believe the fiction from liberal Democrats and certain editorial writers that government must be fed before people, they should come to Ireland. Many expatriates are returning home to find their country as beautiful as ever, but with new economic incentives that make one appreciate the color of money almost as much as the color of the grass on the lovely hills.

MIDDLE EAST:
REALITY TRUMPS HOPE

"The maximum Israel can give is less than
the minimum the Palestinians will take."
—Unidentified Middle East commentator

Since Israel's decisive victory in the Yom Kippur
War, U.S policy has slowly changed from defending
Israel to pressuring it. Now Israel's presence in the
region is regarded as the cause of conflict, which
ignores the centuries of Arab genocide and warfare
before 1948.

Israel has made tangible, critical, painful, and irre-
versible concessions of territory crucial to its sur-
vival. In return, it is promised intangible, vague,
uncertain, and open-ended "guarantees," whose
implementation depends on America's interests, not
Israel's.

The State Department acts as if militant Islamic
fundamentalists can be persuaded to make peace
with people they believe are the enemy of God.

"Our aim is the creation of
a unified and contiguous
Arab region from which Israel
will be eliminated."
—Egyptian President
Gamal Abdul Nasser
(May 15, 1965)

I'll take another look at things when the PLO and the leadership of Arab nations say Allah has changed his mind and no longer views Jews as infidels who must be killed and their land reclaimed solely for Arabs and Muslims.

It isn't up to Israel to make peace, because Israel has never had a charter to obliterate another state or people. It is up to Israel's enemies to make peace, first in their minds and hearts and then on the ground.

This is not about negotiations between equals trying to work out a means by which they might coexist on the same land with mutual respect and guarantees of safety and security. This is about one side's determination to eradicate an entire people from the region by whatever means necessary.

A Palestinian state would not be the end of it. That is a stepping-stone for the eradication of the tiny parcel, roughly the size of Delaware, that would be left of Israel.

Despite mountains of evidence, including documents and covenants in which radical Palestinians and radical Arabs call for the destruction of Israel and the killing of Jews, there are people in high places who exhibit a faith greater than some people's faith in God. Incredibly, they believe that all Israel must do is continue to forfeit land taken for its own security, and if it forfeits enough, Israel's enemies will be persuaded as to Israel's good intentions and will let the Jewish people live in peace. It is as crazy as the unilateral-disarmament crowd that wanted America to throw down its weapons to persuade the Soviet Union we meant them no harm.

Arafat declares: "We won't give up a single grain of our holy land from the sea to the Jordan River." Why is he not believed?

The secular and religious left in the United States, in Israel, and at the *New York Times* continues to feast on the fiction that peace is a matter of process and that what Palestinian leaders and Arabs believe is of no consequence.

> "If peace is to prevail,
> the Palestinians must not have a large army
> equipped with tanks, missiles and artillery,
> a contiguous border with Jordan,
> and the capacity to form alliances
> with such regimes as Iraq and Iran."
> —Prime Minister
> Benjamin Netanyahu
> (May 5, 1999)

President's Clinton remark last week that Palestinians ought to live "wherever they like" ratifies the administration's complete hostility toward the Jewish state and its legitimate security concerns. (July 5, 1999)

If Israel is not secure,
there can be no lasting peace.

Even when buses are bombed and innocent civilians killed, Israel is blamed by most of the world and the press. Arab and Palestinian terror, while sometimes condemned in written statements, is always excused in the context of a people deprived of their "legitimate rights."

No people on earth want peace more than the Jewish people. But they don't want it if it means they must commit suicide. They hate war, but they will fight another one to remain free.

Israel is being squeezed like the Sudetenland before Hitler broke his promise to Neville Chamberlain and launched a war that killed fifty million people, including six million Jews.

The land-for-peace formula was doomed from the start because, while Arafat was happy to take land, he had no intention of granting peace. Why should he when he knows he can get it all with a little patience and a lot of violence?

This year's Palestine Prize for Culture will go to Abu Daoud, mastermind of the 1972 Olympic bombing in Munich that killed eleven Israeli athletes.

*As long as the formula
is "land for peace,"
Israel will give up land
but never get peace.
If the formula is wrong,
the resolution can never be right.*

Every nation pressuring Israel to cede more land and not build in its ancient capital acquired its land and its capital by force from prior "owners." Those nations calling on Israel to divide itself would never think of asking World War I allies to return land seized from the four-hundred-year-old Ottoman Empire, which they awarded to France and which is now called Syria and Lebanon. Why not give Egypt and "Palestine" back to English control? Why shouldn't Turkey demand the liberation of Syria and Iraq, which it once "owned"?

A front-page *New York Times* story asserted that Arafat's police "keep a tight grip on Arab protesters." That is as credible as some of the *Times's* pro-Stalin reporting in the '20s and '30s which claimed that the Soviet dictator was a pretty good guy on balance.

In the twisted reasoning of the Middle East, Israelis are illegal occupiers of land that rightfully belongs to others, and so, when people throw stones and fire weapons, the soldiers fire back and are then saddled with blame.

The PLO was "provoked" long before the beginning of the modern settlements. That's because, for the PLO, Israel's existence is a provocation.

> "The Arab world's antagonism for the West
> raged for a thousand years before Israel
> was added to its list of enemies.
> The Arabs do not hate the West because of Israel;
> they hate Israel because of the West."
> —Benjamin Netanyahu
> (in *A Place Among Nations*)

Diverting blame from Arafat and refusing to hold him responsible for his many violations, including his collaboration with the terrorist Hamas organization, is like treating a serial killer as dysfunctional and sending him to a psychiatrist instead of holding him morally culpable for his acts and sending him to the gallows.

The final irony would come when Jews would be blamed for their own demise for not giving up more territory sooner. It would be explained that the elimination of Israel came as a result of pent-up Arab and Palestinian anger that could not be assuaged.

Imposing a settlement on Israel is the stuff of dictatorship. It isn't how a free nation is supposed to behave. The United States should support democracy, not undermine it. It should be encouraging the parties to negotiate a bottom-up settlement and not trying to impose one from the top down.

This isn't a peace process. It is processed peace which, like processed cheese, can look like the real thing but is full of ingredients that may not contribute to the health of those who swallow it.

Israel's enemies believe the only good Jews are dead Jews. They know how to play the West for suckers. Get ready for the next war. It's coming. The question is whether Israelis will have enough land left to stand and fight and win for the fifth time.

The United States turned away from the Jews once before during World War II. To repeat that error would be an unpardonable sin.

The stage will be set for a war in which Israel's enemies will attack from without and within. The State Department will wring its hands and issue statements saying if only Israel had given up more land earlier, its demise could have been avoided. And then, like Pilate, our government will wash its hands of the whole affair, claiming to be innocent of the blood of the Jewish nation.

As always in the Middle East, reality trumps hope.

Israeli Prime Minister Ehud Barak regrets that he has only one country to give in exchange for his political life.

The United States can afford to be wrong about Arafat's intentions. Israel can't.

ECONOMY AND TRADE:
GIVE FREEDOM A CHANCE

"There is but a fixed quantity
of wealth in this country
at any fixed time.
The only way that we can all secure more of it
is to create more."
—Calvin Coolidge

People are a resource, not a problem. Governments, particularly those that limit freedom and have economic systems that stifle growth, are the problem.

The reason many jobs
have left the country
has more to do with
high taxes and overregulation
than trade policy.

In case no one has noticed, what Democrats now favor for businesses and lower-income residents is the "supply-side economics," or "Reaganomics," they once denounced. For the city of Washington, if not for the nation, Democrats are now promoting the very "bad medicine" they used to reject. It appears to be dawning on them that when rates go down, businesses prosper, profits increase, and so do tax revenues.

*When people are given
the facts and a choice,
the free market wins
over statism every time.*

IMMIGRATION:
EMMA AND ELIAN

The picture of that armed officer pointing his gun at Elian Gonzalez and the fisherman who plucked him from the Atlantic Ocean has already burned into the minds of most people. If this is to be the policy of the U.S. government, let's take the torch from Lady Liberty's hand and replace it with an automatic weapon, cover up the Emma Lazarus poem about sending your tired and poor to our shores, and post a "no trespassing" sign instead. Padlock the Golden Door, because this is not our parents' America.

BELTWAY POLITICS:
FINDING A CURE FOR POTOMAC FEVER

"I'm not sure I want to spend the rest of my life
living in the bubble."
—George W. Bush
(referring to Washington, D.C.)

Sometimes we get so caught up in political and
philosophical divisions that we forget not only the
humanity of those with whom we disagree, but that
we might actually learn something from them if we
take the time to listen.

CONGRESS AND "BIPARTISANSHIP": PICKING POCKETS ACROSS THE AISLE

While Republicans were in the minority in Congress, you could always get a Democrat to pat you on the head and invite you over for drinks so long as you knew your place. Republicans who were prepared to compromise their principles and vote with Democrats would be called civil. It was only when some Republicans, like many of the House freshmen, started standing up for their beliefs and refusing to compromise that they were labeled uncivil for not playing the game.

When the Democrats hold power,
they play rhetorical
and legislative hardball.
When they feel power slipping away,
they talk about reconciliation,
friendship, and redemption.

The history of reconciliation attempts between parties and philosophies which are, at bottom, irreconcilable, has been that the conservatives usually get their ideological pockets picked.

Can anyone remember a time when liberal leaders "reached out" to conservatives and modified their agendas in order to promote civility, understanding, and cooperation? Of course not. As in Israel's negotiations with Palestinians, Republicans are declared civil only when they give up something important to them.

ELECTIONS:
THE BIG CASINO

When ideas are buried, finessed, or discarded during an election season, it is more difficult to raise them the next time around.

All politicians are sometimes forced to make compromises or eat their words in the face of changing realities, but when they compromise on matters of principle and conscience, it is fair to ask whether they stand for anything.

The way to combat cynicism is to do what you promised to do.

President Clinton calls for campaign reform after one of the most tainted fund-raising campaigns in history. This is like having someone who has just punched you in the nose converting to nonviolence before you can defend yourself.

If we are so cynical that we believe all politicians are alike and we demand nothing better, then nothing better is what we will get. Most politicians only rise (or fall) to the expectation levels demanded of them.

*Money without ideas is like
a sports car with no gas.
Ideas drive politics.*

Republicans cannot rely on the press, especially television journalists, to fairly and accurately state their positions, so they must have the money to buy the time to tell their stories themselves.

Fund-raisers of both left and right stoke the coals with ever more outrageous language because only an outraged letter recipient who feels insulted and disenfranchised will send money. Success and kind words are the enemy of a good fund-raising campaign.

The General Accounting Office (GAO) recently published a report that found soft-money contributions by gambling interests to both national

political parties have increased by about 840 percent since 1992. The GAO report also found that
hard-money contributions to federal candidates
from individuals with gambling ties increased by 80
percent during the same period. In other words,
more politicians are being pressured to turn the
United States into one huge casino and politicians
into their wholly owned subsidiaries. Apparently
neither Republican nor Democrat incumbents care
where the money comes from as long as they get
reelected.

ELECTION 2000
AND THE BUTTERFLY BALLOT

*If stupidity were a valid reason
for restaging an election,
we'd be voting every day.*

CORRUPTION AND SCANDALS: WHO SAYS POLITICIANS DON'T HAVE CONVICTIONS?

.

"He who has not a good memory
should never take upon him the trade of lying."
—Michel de Montaigne
(1533–1592)

Democrats, having run out of even bad ideas, have honed their scandal skills instead. These have been their only route to power since Watergate.

Wise parents don't let their kids get away with the "everybody does it" defense. Violating the rules brings punishment. Should we deal with our leaders with less wisdom?

Surely the nation's moral water table has reached drought level when the adulterer, former Senator Gary Hart, feels it's safe to declaim again about whether infidelity should be a factor in determining fitness for public office.

People are always asking me if there are any politicians in Washington with convictions. Yes, I tell them. They're all in federal prison.

Should we demand that only men and women who have never made personal or professional mistakes hold high office? Of course not. But we should not want leaders who pretend there is no standard. There is always room for those who err, confess their guilt, and vow not to repeat their mistakes. This upholds the standard while keeping the door open for redemption. There should be no room for those who claim by their lives and words that there are not, or ought not to be, any foundational principles. They cause harm to their families and their nation.

THE CONSTITUTION VS.
JUDICIAL ACTIVISM

"The Constitution is what the judges say it is."
—Charles Evans Hughes
U.S. Supreme Court Chief Justice
(1862–1948)

We wouldn't need a Constitution at all if unelected, elitist judges could decide everything.

In the presidential debate, Gore advocated designer law which, like fashion, would gratify the changing whims of a population.

"Either the Constitution and statutes are law,
which means that their principles
are known and control judges,
or they are malleable texts that judges
may rewrite to see that particular
groups or political causes win."
—Judge Robert Bork
(in *The Tempting of America*)

Would the liberals be as content to see a conservative court majority causing harm to the Constitution from the right by reading their own biases into the document?

Without being guided by a moral code with a source other than the mind of a judge, what is to keep a judge from becoming a mini-deity? Examples of that self-declared omnipotence have been seen in rulings on school prayer, abortion, and the coming battle over same-sex marriage.

The tyranny of some courts continues.
The will of the majority
and even precedent can be set aside
by the power of a single judge.

BIG GOVERNMENT VS.
INDIVIDUAL FREEDOM

"Power belongs originally to the people,
but if rulers be not well guarded,
that power may be usurped from them."
—William Goudy (1865–1947)

Tyrannies do not pop up overnight. They are a result of a people who grow fat and lazy in their prosperity (or despair) and cede their individual freedom and power to "leaders" who are all too happy to have it.

The Constitution assigns just twenty powers to the national government. All other power was to be diffused: to the states, thousands of counties, tens of thousands of communities, tens of millions of families, and ultimately to hundreds of millions of individual citizens. The Tenth Amendment was specifically written to protect the states from encroaching national government.

Extreme cases are always used by government to force change on the public, which then must succumb to whatever the government wants us to do. Once a precedent is established, it is difficult to stop further government intrusions.

"(The Framers of the Constitution)
knew from vivid,
personal experience that freedom depends on
effective restraints against the accumulation
of power in a single authority.
The root evil is that government
is engaged in activities
in which it has no legitimate business."
—Barry Goldwater
(in *Conscience of a Conservative*)

When politicians tell us the budget has been cut to the bone, they have barely sliced through the skin of the overweight sow known as the federal government.

Ask not what "entitlements"
your government can give to you;
ask what you can do for
yourself and your family.

Name one area where the federal government visits and eventually does not take up permanent residence.

We ask government to do too much and complain when it accomplishes too little. We project on government responsibilities that should first be our own and then lament the loss of community.

Modern national government is viewed by too many as a giant ATM machine, dispensing checks and other goodies for which the slothful do not have to labor.

What do human beings lack that government must give them in order to succeed? More than anything else it is freedom, not to be confused with license.

Our Constitution begins,
"We the people,"
not "we the government."

By saying that government has the tools for success, Clinton implies we cannot be whole or complete without the presence of government in our lives. It isn't true. It never was. The only "tool" we need to succeed is a human spirit unencumbered by government.

If a nation values anything
more than freedom,
it will lose its freedom;
and the irony of it is that if it is
comfort or money that it values more,
it will lose that, too.

Republicans had better start tearing down the wall of big government, or they'll be forced to answer in the next election for behaving like Democrats.

The media enjoy playing up government programs and government regulations, even those that fail, because it isn't the success or failure of these programs that matter, only the intent of those who created and maintain them.

Government will always seek new ways to invade our lives unless it is stopped. It cannot tolerate widespread independent success because if people are successful without government, they will have less need of it.

Supposedly intelligent men and women have grown the federal government as they have tried to perfect humankind through spending on bloated social programs. That they have repeatedly failed never indicates to them that they lack wisdom and that their ideas are wrong, only that their supposed intelligence has not been tried for a sufficient period of time.

"I believe that government should
do a few things and do them well."
—George W. Bush

Government has a legitimate function, but the private sector has one, too, and it is superior. In other words, people are better than institutions.

TAXATION:
WE MAKE IT, THEY TAKE IT

Republicans can't just be against high taxes but for overburdened taxpayers keeping more of their money.

It's our money,
not the government's.
We make it.
They take it.

If people don't mind the government taking up to half of what they make to be used as government wishes, government will continue to grab our money and give us only what it thinks we need.

When government wants to spend your money, it is doing something noble. When you want to keep more of your money, you're greedy.

Reagan repeatedly noted that we have a deficit not because citizens are taxed too little but because government spends too much.

Funny that government can never afford to cut taxes or reduce spending, but taxpayers are never asked whether they can afford higher taxes.

The only way to begin reform is to deprive government of additional money.

Democrats believe government can spend people's money better than the people who earn it.

No one can outpromise, outspend, or outtax better than a liberal Democrat.

Taxpayers spend $20 billion per year on fifteen different federal agencies for job training. Worse, the Government Accounting Office reports that most federal agencies cannot determine the effectiveness of their programs. There are 342 economic development programs managed by thirteen agencies with little or no coordination. At least seventy programs across fifty-seven different departments and agencies receive more than $16 billion a year to fight illegal drug use and yet the "war on drugs" is being won by the drug lords. Now what was that again about government not being able to "afford" a tax cut? The question should be, can we who pay the bills afford any more of this wasteful, fraudulent, and abusive government?

The pretax price of gasoline at the pump barely changed between 1990 and 2000, actually declining from eighty-eight cents per gallon to eighty-six cents as of last November. But over that same period, state and federal gasoline taxes jumped from twenty-seven cents per gallon to forty-three cents.

The American people should be telling government how much of our money we think it needs to do the job the people want done and how much of our money we intend to let government have. Government should not be telling us how much of our money it intends to let us keep.

But this is government,
which never has to say it's sorry,
reform its ways, or give us
our money back.

The bargain I have with government is that I send them up to half my income, and in return they promise not to put me in jail. God asks for only 10 percent. The total government take is 50 percent. Wouldn't more get done if the numbers were reversed?

GUNS & SUVS:
UNCLE SAM WANTS YOU!

Attorney General Janet Reno, Vice President Al(pha) Gore, the big media, and the usual suspects in the antigun lobby won't be satisfied until the only people with access to guns are criminals.

Evidence in countries where gun laws tougher than ours exist show more, not less, crime. In Great Britain, where massive firearms-confiscation programs were enacted following a widely publicized shooting in Scotland, gun-related crimes have increased,

including "hot" robberies, meaning those conducted while the victims are at home. Criminals apparently believe their odds have improved since many of the law-abiding people have been disarmed.

Let's maintain freedom of choice on what vehicles people can buy. Government already mandates seat belts, air bags, bumper styles, and gasoline consumption. Don't let it reduce the safety level of pickups and SUVs.

WELFARE REFORM AND POVERTY RELIEF:
"THE WORK OF A NATION"

"Compassion is the work of a nation,
not just a government."
—George W. Bush
(in his Inaugural Address)

It is not enough to support a welfare reform bill. We must also mentor the children of poverty who live without fathers and without hope.

Charity and compassion should begin at home, not with government.

What is more likely to happen as a result of welfare reform is that those who have made poverty their profession will be making a career change. (August 26, 1996)

The Clinton administration gave volunteerism a bad name when it established "AmeriCorps" and paid the "volunteers."

Much of government's answer to poverty has been the equivalent of a topical solution to an internal disease.

Does it make sense that a government program (food stamps) that provides a paltry $150 a month to recipients pays employees who administer the program between $30,000 and $150,000 per year?

It would be a most welcome trend—in Britain and America—if people would begin to see government aid as a last stop, not the first stop, and the moral resuscitation of people as the honorable obligation of the churches and not primarily of the government.

SOCIAL SECURITY:
OUR THIRD WORLD RETIREMENT PLAN

Flash! Workers no longer have to worry about whether they will have enough money to sustain them in retirement. The problem has been fixed without reducing benefits and without raising taxes. That would be good news if it was about America. Unfortunately, the news is about Sweden, Mexico, Great Britain, even Poland and many other countries where some form of privatization is far outpacing state-run pension systems.

*Why does the United States,
which is pioneering in technology,
remain in the Dark Ages when
it comes to retirement?*

Once people realize how well other countries are doing and how poorly they will do by comparison, they will opt for the plan that gives them more money for their own retirement.

According to the World Bank, every Latin American country, except Cuba, will have a private retirement system this year. Why are these countries headed toward the First World and we are behaving like a Third World nation and even continuing to tax Social Security benefits?

HEALTH-CARE RX:
MEDICAL SAVINGS ACCOUNTS

Serious Social Security and Medicare reform will work, but the truth is Democrats want to use the issue against Republicans rather than solve the problems. That way they can continue their slander of Republicans as uncaring about the elderly and the poor. But true compassion means fixing something that is broken so that it will benefit the people it was designed to serve.

*Health care doesn't need
federal micromanagement.
Expanding choice,
not expanding the currently
flawed system,
is the best way to improve access
to and quality of health care.*

President Clinton wants to allow people as young as fifty-five to buy into the Medicare system, yet interest-bearing medical savings accounts holding an insured's own money would reduce the size of government and expand coverage choices for us all.

The lie is that Medicare needs more money. The truth is it needs comprehensive fixing. There are more than 111,000 pages of rules and regulations governing Medicare patients. The answer to the problems surrounding Medicare is a system of choices, allowing families to pick the plans that provide the benefits they need, not a government bureaucracy that imposes a one-size-fits-all program.

" I'M SORRY BUT YOU CAN HAVE BRONCHITIS ONLY ON EVEN MONDAYS... WOULD YOU LIKE TO SWITCH TO KIDNEY STONES OR PNEUMONIA? "

PART THREE

Hollywood and the Media

THE ARTS:
BEAUTY AND THE BEAST

It only takes a moment to feel clean. It makes me wonder why some people fixate on the dark and ugly beast when we could be more profitably and wonderfully engaged in the creation and encouragement of beauty.

While the rest of television is immersed in sex and sleaze, *Touched by an Angel* continues to prove that a show committed to virtue, that encourages people to seek higher and better things, cannot only

"JUDGING BY WHAT I'VE BEEN SEEING ON TV, I'D SAY HE'S BEEN DEAD ABOUT 12 TO 15 YEARS!"

survive in the vast video wasteland but prevail. Watch this show! Be inspired, be blessed, and be motivated to do something that can touch and improve lives. As Executive Producer Martha Williamson has noted, we have all been given the power to do one good thing.

"HERE IT IS. A CLEANED-UP VERSION OF MADONNA'S LATEST VIDEO... 4/10THS OF A SECOND OF REAL GOOD STUFF!"

BROADWAY:
THE LULLABY HAS BEEN PUT TO SLEEP

Modernists, who haven't done too well creating hit Broadway musicals in recent years, are now tinkering with the classics, trying to exorcise them of racial and ethnic stereotypes. Fortunately, Producer Hal Prince resisted the pressure and presented the original book, music, and lyrics in his fabulous revival of Jerome Kern's *Showboat*. Prince rejected criticism from some civil rights groups about racial stereotyping (these are some of the same people who want to censure Mark Twain and object to a recent book about "nappy hair," even though it is a positive work authored by a black woman). Not overly gifted with creative skills, some try to diminish others who are.

The lullaby of Broadway has itself been put to sleep. In its place is a lot of hack work and mostly bad revivals that resurrect like unresuscitated corpses.

MEDIA SLANT: "WHAT, ME BIASED?"

"It is impossible to be objective,
so we must always try to be fair."
—David Brinkley

Reporters and commentators have an obligation to understand the terms and beliefs of persons about whom they write. They don't have to believe in the same things to do their job well, but accuracy and fairness ought to be expected.

The networks just don't get it.
They're losing market share because
those they regularly offend
in their one-sided reporting
have tuned out.

Dan Rather said that "Castro feels a very deep and abiding connection" to the Cuban people. Maybe that's why he has so many of them in prison and in graves, so he will always have them close by.

"If we could be one-hundredth as great as you
and Hillary Rodham Clinton have been in the
White House, we'd take it right now and
walk away winners."
— Dan Rather on CBS
(May 27, 1993)

On *Larry King Live* a few weeks ago, several television journalists (but no critics) were interviewed,
and all denied they slanted the news. I guess that
settles it, then. It's all in our minds, not theirs.

No other company functions like the media. If you
own a fast-food chain and the customers begin
drifting away, you quickly find out what has turned
them off and what will bring them back. Not with
the big media. They would rather go out of business
than offer fair, accurate, and balanced reporting
and viewpoints.

The last time I wrote something critical about a
network on which I appeared, they banned me. I
haven't been on ABC since I criticized *Good
Morning America* for disinviting me because a producer feared I might quote a Bible verse. It was the
ultimate exercise of prior restraint.

After years of complaining about liberally slanted and distorted news coverage, only to have the networks deny such bias, the people are voting the only way they know how. They are tuning out and turning off.

Today's thinly disguised editorializing is frequently done on the front page and in statements by network anchors and morning-show hosts that are designed to stroke the ones they support and confront those they oppose.

If politicians are invading broadcast news, and if some in broadcast news use the medium as their personal "holding pattern" to maintain visibility until the next election, how is the public served? How do they know what they're getting is really the news and not "spin"?

The public is being asked to accept global warming without a debate. When global-warming opponents attempt to speak, they are mostly ignored or, as on a recent *Nightline* broadcast, put down by the usually fair Ted Koppel as ignorant members of the Flat Earth Society.

Mislabeled "breaking news" revealed how broken the news has become. The Television People stopped the world, but they didn't want to get off. A once-proud profession has become all tabloid, all the time. A profession mostly respected in the past, which once informed, now merely titillates.

It wasn't just the news cycle that frustrated the Starr investigation. It was the way television hosts, anchors, and reporters served as surrogate defense counsels for the president to their everlasting shame and the diminishment of their profession.

> "Mr. President, we love you.
> I want to hug you."
> —Geraldo Rivera
> on MSNBC
> (during the Clinton impeachment coverage)

Because religion is so intertwined with contemporary politics, newsrooms ought to include people on their staffs who believe as millions of Americans do and who can report correctly and fairly on those beliefs in a way that will inform all of us.

The commentators, analysts, and questioners also betray their biases by their assumptions. They assume that the standard is gay rights, abortion rights, high taxes, huge spending, and big government. It seems to be taken for granted that Democratic positions form the benchmark by which all other politicians should be measured.

Most of the big media subscribe to certain prejudices. They include, but are not limited to, biases about big corporations (they are evil), white people (they are racists until proved otherwise), males (they are sexists), Republicans (they are shills for big business and insensitive to the poor), the seriously religious (they are ignorant), and America (a bad country that does bad things to innocent people).

When the media speak of "diversity," they are not talking about diversity of opinion, only different faces and genders delivering the same one-sided viewpoint.

There are many ways to lie or "shade the truth" in the news profession. The most extreme cases can get you fired. The less extreme can win you an award.

Much of the press labors under an Alfred E. Newman philosophy of "What, me biased?"

If most of journalism supports a liberal Democrat view of the world, what difference will it make in ratings and credibility if that liberalism comes from the mouth or from the pen of an African American, Native American, Hispanic, or Asian journalist? A liberal is a liberal no matter what his or her make-up. True diversity would be represented in story selection, ideological balance, and the diverse beliefs of America. It would be a journalism that not only looks like America, but believes like Americans.

Being part of the big media means never having to get it right.

The reason the *New York Times* and their fellow ideological travelers cannot bring themselves to credit Reagan, Thatcher, and the Pope for what they did [to bring down the Soviet empire] is that they would have, in the words of Desi Arnaz, "a lot of 'splainin' to do."

No one ever got into trouble with the public for dissing the press. Columnist Steve Dunleavy reminds us about a truly great insulter, Harry Truman, who told off a newspaperman for writing a bad review of daughter Margaret's performance in a vocal and piano recital. Truman threatened to punch him in the nose and in a far more sensitive place for males. The public loved it.

The networks have all pledged to establish panels to look into their election-night coverage and recommend how they can do better. That sounds like a good start until you realize that only CBS has an outsider on its panel—the respected Kathleen Hall Jamieson, Dean of the Annenberg School for Communication at the University of Pennsylvania. The rest are all using network insiders. This is like the Justice Department investigating itself, which is why we once had an Independent Counsel law.

One change the networks can make immediately is to stop hiring operatives from Republican and Democrat camps as "commentators," "analysts," and reporters, such as George Stephanopoulos. The network downplays Stephanopoulos's ties to Clinton-Gore. He's a "correspondent" now, you see, because ABC brass says so.

Media culpability in the 2000 presidential election goes beyond the bad network calls. The networks, especially, suffer from bias denial and falling credibility that ill serves the public at a time when truth and accuracy were never more needed.

Jesse Jackson will not suffer the same ostracism and rejection experienced by Bakker and Swaggart. The reasons are that he is treated differently by liberals in the media, and that anyone who criticizes a black person for even legitimate reasons runs the risk of being called a racist, a charge against which it is nearly impossible to defend yourself. Ask John Ashcroft. (This comment followed the revelation that Rev. Jesse Jackson had fathered a child out of wedlock with an employee with whom he was having an affair.)

MEDIA INFLUENCE:
VULGARIANS AND BARBARIANS

"I'm always surprised to hear politicians
promoting the agenda of the Hollywood elites.
If there's anybody whose agenda needs promoting,
it is the middle-class American family."
—Dan Quayle

*Which is the more extreme
family role model:
Ozzie and Harriet
or Beavis and Butthead?*

Most television has become like cigarettes. The content is so poisonous that labeling the product does nothing to help those who are irresponsible enough to ingest it. My prediction is that those who break the TV habit will never go back and will find that, like those who quit smoking, they'll have a better life.

Oliver Stone says he would now think twice before directing a movie with explicit sexual content because of the editing policy at Wal-Mart and the other big chains. Good. That's the idea.

> *What good does it do*
> *to hook kids up to computers*
> *if it merely speeds up the process*
> *by which they receive bad ideas?*

The tobacco companies make products that kill the body. The networks spew forth material that poisons the mind and soul.

NEWS: TV NETWORKS TO LIMIT VIOLENCE.

As Steve Allen put it, television affords an opportunity for vulgarians to address barbarians. Labeling the programs doesn't make them less harmful any more than labeling cigarettes protects smokers.

Television has reduced our attention span, watered down family conversation, and separated households. Much of TV programming resembles the planet Mars—barren, with an unfriendly atmosphere.

Television teaches through images, words, and situations. It gives permission for people to be good or bad. Each must make his or her own choice, but television can reinforce good choices and show the error of bad ones.

Parents who take their young daughters to see such things as the Spice Girls are accessories in eroding their daughters' innocence, in complicity with the sex educators in many of the government schools. Girls are being herded at earlier ages into attitudes and practices far from the "sugar and spice and everything nice" we used to think, or at least wished, that little girls were made of.

The NFL should extend its rule against crude gestures to include bad language, on the field and while representing professional football during postgame interviews.

The government must also do something about praying players who offend some fans and sports writers. In the interest of tolerance and diversity, players should address their prayers to "to whom it may concern." Players who mention Jesus in postgame interviews will be told they can use the name only while cursing.

Television is now banal at best and more often offensive to those who seek stimulation outside their erogenous zones. A recent *Cosmopolitan* magazine tells young women how to "unleash" their lusts. I was not aware that *Cosmo* readers ever had their lusts leashed.

Some parents may have to conduct search-and-destroy missions in their teenager's room, tearing down posters that depict violence and sex, throwing out music CDs with violent and hate-filled lyrics.

We are awash in pornography, but fewer corporations are principled enough to resist temptation and serve as positive examples. We hear a lot about "corporate responsibility" when it comes to pollution and the environment. What about some corporate responsibility when it comes to polluting the mind and soul?

For decades we have been told that the price we all must pay for a healthy First Amendment is the toleration of the most disgusting filth oozing through every pore of our society and culture. Creeps, louts, pornographers, blasphemers, alternative life-stylers, fornicators, adulterers, liars, slanderers, and other forms of human rubbish enjoy the full protection of the law.

P.S. Would news directors please get street reporters to stop turning around? It's television. We see what's behind you!

CELEBRITIES:
IN BRIEF MEMORIAM

STEVE ALLEN
(1921–2000)

The great comedians were never dirty. You could always invite them into your home without fear that they would soil your reputation or singe your ears. Steve Allen, who died Tuesday at the age of seventy-eight, was the greatest of the great. He never told a dirty joke on television. He didn't have to. He had talent. (10/31/00)

PRINCESS DIANA
(1961–1997)

The plot of Diana's life—from beaming princess at her fairy-tale royal wedding to a mangled body inside the twisted wreckage of a luxury car in a Paris tunnel—is a tragedy of Shakespearean proportion.

The accessories in Diana's death are members of the royal family, who never appeared to welcome her and who constantly sought to make her over into their dull, dowdy, and dysfunctional image.

Charles didn't have the class or character to be worthy of his wife. She had her problems, but all probably could have been overcome (or never started) with loving attention from a husband devoted to her and not his mother, the monarchy, and his mistress. He does not deserve the throne of England.

ROY ROGERS
(1911–1998)

On many occasions I have eaten lunch at Roy Rogers, but not until last December had I ever had lunch with Roy Rogers. It was the eve of the Rogers's fiftieth wedding anniversary. Roy and Dale Evans Rogers had graciously agreed to meet with my wife and me at their museum in Victorville, California, indulging my childhood wish to see the King of the Cowboys and Queen of the West.

For those not of a certain age, it will be difficult to understand the influence that Roy and Dale had on America's children in the '50s. Yes, we first learned right from wrong at home from our parents, but Roy and Dale and so many other programs either reinforced or at least did not damage that moral standard.

So there I was, sitting across from one of my childhood heroes. Roy was used to this. He played his part perfectly. The clothes were cowboy, including the hat. Those wonderful eyes that always smiled looked directly into mine and I felt like a child again.

Roy has now joined his children, Robin, Debbie, and Sandy, at the end of his final and happiest trail of all. Happy trails, Roy, 'til we meet again.

(July 7, 1998)

LORETTA YOUNG
(1913–2000)

Today there are celebrities in abundance, but there are few true stars. Loretta was a star. I saw her stop conversation as she entered a room. Everyone who met her knows what I mean. And we know that what Lord Byron wrote about another woman in another century could well be applied to Loretta:

She walks in beauty, like the night
Of cloudless climes and starry skies;
And all that's best of dark and bright
Meet in her aspect and her eyes.

(August 15, 2000)

ABOUT THE AUTHOR

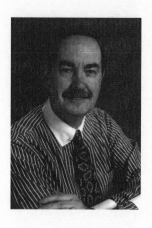 Cal Thomas is the author of *The Things That Matter Most, Uncommon Sense,* and *Occupied Territory,* and coauthor of *Blinded by Might* with Dr. Edward Dobson and *Liberals for Lunch* (with Stayskal). His twice-weekly column is distributed by Tribune Media Services. Appearing in more than 500 newspapers, it is the most widely syndicated political column in the country. Cal and his wife, Ray, live in Alexandria, Virginia.